IN THE NAME OF
ALLAH
THE ALL-COMPASSIONATE, ALL-MERCIFUL

The True Message of
Jesus Christ

- Title: *The True Message of Jesus Christ*
- Author: Dr. Abu Ameenah Bilal Philips
- New Revised Edition 2 (2006)
- Layout: IIPH, Riyadh, Saudi Arabia
- Filming & Cover Designing: Samo Press Group

The True Message of
Jesus Christ

الرسالة الحقيقية لعيسى عليه السلام

Dr. Abu Ameenah Bilal Philips

INTERNATIONAL ISLAMIC PUBLISHING HOUSE

© **International Islamic Publishing House, 2006**

King Fahd National Library Cataloging-in-Publication Data

Philips, Abu Ameenah Bilal
   The true message of Jesus Christ / Abu Ameenah Bilal Philips -
Riyadh , 2006

   ...p ; 22 cm

   ISBN : **9960-850-82-X**

   1- Jesus Christ   I-Title

   273.2 dc   1424/6810

ISBN: **9960-850-82-X**
Legal deposit no. 1424/6810

International Islamic Publishing House (IIPH)
P.O.Box 55195 Riyadh 11534, Saudi Arabia
Tel: 966 1 4650818 - 4647213 - Fax: 4633489
E-Mail: iiph@iiph.com.sa - www.iiph.com.sa

TABLE OF CONTENTS

TRANSLITERATION CHART

أ	a
آ . ى	â
ب	b
ت	t
ة	h or t (when followed by another Arabic word)
ث	th
ج	j
ح	ḥ
خ	kh
د	d
ذ	dh
ر	r
ز	z
س	s
ش	sh
ص	ṣ
ض	ḍ
ط	ṭ

ظ	<u>dh</u>
ع	‘
غ	gh
ف	f
ق	q
ك	k
ل	l
م	m
ن	n
ھ – ه – ہ – ـه	h
و	w
و (as vowel)	oo
ي	y
ي (as vowel)	ee
ء	’
	(Omitted in initial position)

´	Fatḥah	a
´	Kasrah	i
ُ	Ḍammah	u
ّ	Shaddah	Double letter
°	Sukoon	Absence of vowel

INTRODUCTION

J esus Christ represents the common link between the two major religions (having the most followers) on earth today — Christianity and Islam. The following study of Jesus' message and his personality is based on this link. It is hoped that through this study, both Muslims and Christians will better understand the significance of Jesus and the importance of his message.

However, for us to accurately identify the true message of Jesus Christ, an objective point of view must be maintained throughout the course of our research. We should not allow our emotions to cloud our vision and thereby blind us from the truth. We must look at all of the issues rationally and separate the truth from falsehood — with the help of the Almighty.

When we look at the variety of false religions and deviant beliefs around the world and the zeal with which their followers uphold these beliefs, it becomes quite evident that these people are not able to find the truth because of their blind commitment to their beliefs. Their tenacious adherence is usually not based on an intellectual understanding of the teachings, but on powerful cultural and emotional influences. Because they were raised in a particular family or society, they firmly cling to the beliefs of that society, believing that they are upholding the truth.

The only way that we can find the truth about any subject (topic) is to approach it systematically and logically. First, we weigh the evidence and then we judge it by the intelligence which God has given us. In the material world, it is fundamentally intelligence that distinguishes humans from animals, which act purely on instinct. After determining what the objective truth is, we must then commit ourselves to it emotionally. Yes, there is a place for emotional commitment, but emotional commitment must come after a reasoned comprehension of the issues. Emotional commitment is essential, because it is evidence of true understanding. When one fully and properly understands the reality of the issue, he is then mentally and spiritually prepared to vigorously uphold that reality.

It is from this intellectual and spiritual point of view that the subject of Jesus' message and his relevance to those who desire to follow God will be analyzed in the following pages.

Dr. Abu Ameenah Bilal Philips

CHAPTER ONE

THE SCRIPTURES

The topic *The True Message of Jesus Christ* is comprised of two basic parts of Jesus Christ: **a)** the person and **b)** his message. Each one is inseparable from the other. In order to understand Jesus' message, we must know who he was. However, for us to understand who he was, it is also necessary to identify and comprehend his message.

There are two possible avenues which may be taken to look into the identity of Jesus Christ and the content of his message. One is based on the historical record compiled by modern historians from the writings and relics of that period and the other is based on the reports contained in the revealed Scriptures.

In reality, there is very little historical evidence available to inform us about who Jesus Christ was or to determine what his message was. The official historical documents of that time contain virtually no record of Jesus. A biblical scholar, R.T. France, writes, "No 1st century inscription mentions him and no object or building has survived which has a specific link to him."[1] This fact has even led some Western historians to mistakenly claim that Jesus Christ never actually existed. Therefore, research

---

[1] Time, December 18, 1995, p. 46.

has to be primarily based on the scriptures which address the person and the mission of Jesus Christ. The scriptures in question are those officially recognized by both Christianity and Islam. However, to accurately analyze the information contained in these religious texts, it is essential to first determine their validity. Are they reliable sources of documentary evidence, or humanly concocted tales and myths, or a mixture of both? Are the Bible's Old and New Testaments divinely revealed scriptures? Is the Qur'an (Koran) authentic?

For the Bible and the Qur'an to be the divine word of God, they must be free from inexplicable contradictions, and there should be no doubt about their content nor about their authors. If this is the case, the material contained in the Old and New Testaments and the Qur'an can then be considered reliable sources of information concerning the message and the person of Jesus Christ.

Authentic manuscripts

It has been documented by many scholars from various branches and sects of Christianity that much of the material in the Bible is of doubtful authenticity.

In the preface of *The Myth of God Incarnate,* the editor wrote the following: "In the nineteenth century, Western Christianity made two major new adjustments in response to important enlargements of human knowledge: it accepted that man is a part of nature and has emerged within the evolution of the forms of life on this earth; and it accepted that the books of the Bible were written by a variety of human beings in a variety of circumstances, and cannot be accorded a verbal divine authority."[2]

---

[2] *The Myth of God Incarnate,* p. ix.

In the international news magazine, *Newsweek*[3] which carried an article entitled *'O' Lord, Who Wrote Thy Prayer?'*, a group of theologians from the major Protestant sects, along with noted Roman Catholic Biblical scholars in the United States, after a detailed examination of the earliest manuscripts of the New Testament, concluded that the only words of the "Lord's prayer"[4] that can be accurately attributed to Jesus Christ is "father". That is, according to these learned church scholars, all the words that came after the beginning phrase, "Our father", of the most fundamental Christian prayer, were added centuries later by church scribes who copied the early manuscripts of the Gospels.[5] U.S. News & World Report, further quotes the team of scholars as saying that over 80 percent of the words ascribed to Jesus in the Gospels may be apocryphal[6]. That includes Jesus' Eucharistic[7] speech at the Last Supper ("Take, eat. This is my body...") and every word he is said to have uttered from the cross.[8]

Dr. J. K. Elliott, of the Department of Theology and Religious Studies at Leeds University, wrote an article published in *The Times,* London (10th Sept., 1987) entitled "Checking the Bible's Roots". In it, he stated that: "More than 5,000 manuscripts

---

[3] October 31, 1988, p. 44.

[4] Luke 11:2 and Matthew 6:9-10.

[5] The word gospel is derived from the Anglo-Saxon term god-spell, meaning "good story," a rendering of the Latin *evangelium* and the Greek *euangelion*, meaning "good news" or "good telling." (*The New Encyclopaedia Britannica*, vol. 5, p. 379).

[6] Apocryphal: not likely to be genuine; untrue or invented. (*Oxford Advanced Learner's Dictionary*, p. 45).

[7] The Eucharist is the bread and wine taken at the Christian ceremony based on Christ's last supper. (*Oxford Advanced Learner's Dictionary*, p. 410.)

[8] July 1, 1991, p. 57.

contain all or part of the New Testament in its original language. These range in date from the second century up to the invention of printing. It has been estimated that no two agree in all particulars. Inevitably, all handwritten documents are liable to contain accidental errors in copying. However, in living theological works it is not surprising that deliberate changes were introduced to avoid or alter statements that the copyist found unsound. There was also a tendency for copyists to add explanatory glosses[9]. Deliberate changes are more likely to have been introduced at an early stage before the canonical status of the New Testament was established."

The author went on to explain that "no one manuscript contains the original, unaltered text in its entirety," and that, "one cannot select any one of these manuscripts and rely exclusively on its text as if it contained the monopoly of the original words of the original authors." He further said: "If one further argues that the original text has survived somewhere among the thousands of extant[10] manuscripts, then one is forced to read all these manuscripts, to assemble the differences between them in a systematic way, and then to assess, variant by variant, which manuscripts have the original (text) and which the secondary text. Such a prospect has daunted[11] many biblical scholars who have been content to rely on the printed texts of earlier ages, in which the evidence of only a few favoured manuscripts were used. Even many recent printed editions of the Greek New Testament, and modern translations based on these, usually follow this practice of

---

[9] A 'gloss' is an explanatory comment added to a text; brief definition. (*Oxford Advanced Learner's Dictionary*, p. 528).

[10] extant: Surviving, in existence

[11] Daunted discouraged, frightened.

building their text on a narrow base that is unlikely to be entirely original."

Versions of the English Bible

In the preface of the most widely used version of the Bible, the *Revised Standard Version,* the authors wrote the following:

The Revised Standard Version of the Bible is an authorized revision of the *American Standard Version,* published in 1901, which was a revision of the *King James Version,* published in 1611...

"The *King James Version* had to compete with the *Geneva Bible* (1560) in popular use; but in the end it prevailed, and for more than two and a half centuries no other authorized translation of the Bible into English was made. *The King James Version* became the 'Authorized Version' of the English-speaking peoples... Yet the *King James Version* has grave defects. By the middle of the nineteenth century, the development of Biblical studies and the discovery of many manuscripts more ancient than those upon which the *King James Version* was based, made it manifest that these defects are **so many and so serious** as to call for revision of the English translation. The task was undertaken, by authority of the Church of England, in 1870. The *English Revised Version* of the Bible was published in 1881-1885; and the *American Standard Version,* its variant embodying the preferences of the American scholars associated in the work, was published in 1901."[12]

---

[12] *The Holy Bible: Revised Standard Version,* p. iii.

"The *King James Version* of the New Testament was based upon a Greek text that was marred by mistakes, containing the accumulated errors of fourteen centuries of manuscript copying. It was essentially the Greek text of the New Testament as edited by Beza, 1589, who closely followed that published by Erasmus, 1516-1535, which was based upon a few medieval manuscripts. The earliest and best of the eight manuscripts which Erasmus consulted was from the **tenth century**, and he made the least use of it because it differed most from the commonly received text; Beza had access to two manuscripts of great value, dating from the fifth and sixth centuries, but he made very little use of them because they differed from the text published by Erasmus." [13]

"...The *American Standard Version* was copyrighted, to protect the text from unauthorized changes. In 1928 this copyright was acquired by the International Council of Religious Education, and thus passed into the ownership of the churches of the United States and Canada which were associated in this Council through their boards of education and publication. The Council appointed a committee of scholars to have charge of the text of the *American Standard Version* and to undertake inquiry as to whether further revision was necessary... (After two years) the decision was reached that there is need for a thorough revision of the version of 1901, which will stay as close to the *Tyndale-King James* tradition as it can... In 1937 the revision was authorized by vote of the Council." [14]

"Thirty-two scholars have served as members of the Committee charged with making the revision, and they have

---

[13] *The Holy Bible: Revised Standard Version*, p. v.

[14] Ibid., p. iii-iv.

secured the review and counsel of an Advisory Board of fifty representatives of the co-operating denominations... The *Revised Standard Version* of the New Testament was published in 1946."[15] "The *Revised Standard Version* of the Bible, containing the Old and New Testaments, was published on September 30, 1952, and was met with wide acceptance."[16]

In the *Revised Standard Version* of the Bible, a number of key verses from the *King James Version* of the Old and the New Testaments, which Biblical scholars concluded, and which were added in later centuries, were removed from the text and placed in the footnotes. For example, the famous passage in the Gospel of John 8.7 about an adulteress who was about to be stoned. Jesus was supposed to have said: *"Let him who is without sin among you be the first to throw a stone at her."* The footnotes of the *Revised Standard Version* of the Bible (1952) state "The most ancient authorities omit 7.53-8.11".[17] Since the Vatican manuscript no. 1209 and the Sinaitic manuscript codex from the 4th century do not contain these twelve verses, Biblical scholars have concluded that these words cannot be attributed to Jesus. Another example is the passage attributed to Jesus and used as evidence of reference to the Trinity in the Scriptures. In 1 John 5.7, Jesus was supposed to have said : *"There are three that bear record in heaven, the Father, the Word, and the Holy Ghost: and these three are one."*[18] The well known Biblical scholar, Benjamin Wilson, writes that this text concerning the "heavenly witness" is not contained in any Greek manuscript which was written earlier than the 15th century! Consequently, in the *Revised Standard Version*, <u>this verse was</u>

---

[15] *The Holy Bible: Revised Standard Version*, p. iv.

[16] Ibid., p. vi.

[17] Ibid., p. 96.

[18] *Holy Bible*: (*King James Version*).

deleted from the text without even so much as a footnote. However, in order to keep the total number of verses in the *Revised Standard version* the same as that of the *King James version*, the revisers split verse 6 into two verses.

The Second Edition of the translation of the New Testament (1971) profited from textual and linguistic studies published since the *Revised Standard Version* New Testament was first issued in 1946.[19] Consequently, some previously deleted passages were reinstated, and some accepted passages were deleted. "Two passages, the longer ending of Mark (16.9-20) and the account of the woman caught in adultery (John 7.53-8.11), were restored to the text, separated from it by a blank space and accompanied by informative notes... With new manuscript support, two passages, Luke 22.19b-20 and 24.51b, were restored to the text, and one passage, Luke 22.43-44, was placed in the footnotes, as was a phrase in Luke 12.39."[20]

Authorship

According to Biblical scholars, even the authorship of the Old Testament books and the Gospels themselves is in doubt.

Torah

The first five books of the Bible (the Pentateuch)[21] are traditionally attributed to Prophet Moses,[22] however, there are

---

[19] *The Holy Bible: Revised Standard Version*, p. vi.

[20] Ibid., p. vii.

[21] Genesis, Exodus, Leviticus, Numbers and Deuteronomy.

[22] Orthodox Jews claim that the Torah, the Jewish name for the first five books, was created 974 generations before the creation of the world. According=

many verses within these books which indicate that Prophet Moses could not possibly have written everything in them. For example, Deuteronomy 34.5-8 states: "**5** *So Moses the servant of the Lord died there in the land of Moab, according to the word of the Lord,* **6** *and he buried him in the valley of the land of Moab opposite Beth-peor; but no man knows the place of his burial to this day.* **7** *Moses was a hundred and twenty years old when he died; his eye was not dim, nor his natural force abated.* **8** *And the people of Israel wept for Moses in the plains of Moab thirty days; then the days of weeping and mourning for Moses ended.*" It is quite obvious that someone else wrote these verses about Prophet Moses' death.

Some Christian scholars have explained these discrepancies by suggesting that Moses had written his books, but that later prophets, as well as inspired scribes, had made the additions previously mentioned. Consequently, according to them, the text, in its entirety, remained an inspired scripture of God. However, this explanation did not stand up to scrutiny, because the style and literary characteristics of the interpolated verses are the same as the remainder of the text.

In the 19th century, Christian Bible scholars began to debate the meaning of "doublets" that appeared in the Torah. These are stories which appear twice, each time with different details. Among these are the two versions of the creation of the world, of the covenant between God and Abraham, of God changing Jacob's name to Israel and of Moses getting water from a rock.[23]

=to them, God dictated the Torah during the 40 days Moses was on Mount Sinai, in such a final and irrevocable form that it is sinful to claim that Moses wrote even one letter of it by himself.

[23] *Who Wrote the Bible*, Pp. 54-70.

Defenders of Moses' authorship said that the doublets were not contradictory, but instructive. Their intent was to teach us about the deeper, more subtle meanings of the Torah. However, this claim was soon brushed aside by open-minded scholars who noted that, not only were some accounts clearly contradictory, but also that when the doublets were separated into two separate accounts, each account consistently used a different name for God. One would always refer to God as *Yahweh / Jehovah*, This document was called "J". The other always referred to God as *Elohim,* and was called "E".[24] There were various other literary characteristics found to be common to one document or the other. Modern linguistic analyses, according to Professor Richard Friedman,[25] indicate that the five books of Moses are a mixture of Hebrew from the ninth, eighth, seventh and sixth centuries B.C. Therefore, Moses, who was alive in the 13th century B.C., was further away from the Hebrew of the Bible than Shakespeare was from the English of today.

Further study of the Pentateuch led to the discovery that it was not made up of two major sources but of four. It was discovered that some stories were not only doublets but triplets. Additional literary characteristics were identified for these documents. The third source was called "P" (for priestly), and the fourth called "D" (for Deuteronomy).[26]

---

[24] The late 19th century German scholar, Julius Wellhausen, was the first to identify the multiple sources for the five books.

[25] Richard Elliot Friedman is a professor in the University of California at San Diego. He earned his Doctorate in Hebrew Bible at Harvard University, and is the author of the controversial work, *Who Wrote the Bible.*

[26] *The Interpreter's Dictionary of the Bible,* vol. 1, p. 756, and vol. 3, p. 617. See also *The New Encyclopaedia Britannica,* vol. 14, Pp. 773-4.

The extent to which less obvious additions were made to the original text is very difficult to determine. Consequently, a great shadow of doubt has been cast on the authorship of the books as a whole.

In the appendix of the *Revised Standard Version* entitled "Books of the Bible," the following is written concerning the authorship of over one third of the remaining books of the Old Testament:

Books	Authors
Judges	Possibly Samuel
Ruth	Perhaps Samuel
First Samuel	Unknown
Second Samuel	Unknown
First Kings	Unknown
Second Kings	Unknown

Books	Authors
First Chronicles	Unknown
Esther	Unknown
Job	Unknown
Ecclesiastes	Doubtful
Jonah	Unknown
Malachi	Nothing known

Apocrypha

More than half of the world's Christians are Roman Catholics. Their version of the Bible was published in 1582 from Jerome's Latin Vulgate, and reproduced at Douay in 1609. The Old Testament of the RCV (*Roman Catholic Version*) contains <u>seven more books</u> than the *King James Version* recognized by the Protestant world. The extra books are referred to as the *apocrypha* (i.e., of doubtful authority) and were removed from the Bible in 1611 by Protestant Bible scholars.

The Gospels

Aramaic was the spoken language of the Jews of Palestine. Consequently, it is believed that Jesus and his disciples spoke and taught in Aramaic.[27] "The earliest oral tradition of Jesus' deeds and sayings undoubtedly circulated in Aramaic. However, the four Gospels were written in an entirely different speech, common Greek, the spoken language of the civilized Mediterranean world, to serve the majority of the Church, which was becoming Hellenistic (Greek-speaking) instead of Palestinian. Traces of Aramaic survive in the Greek Gospels. For example, in Mark 5:41, "*Taking her by the hand he said to her, 'Tal'itha cu'mi'; which means 'Little girl, I say to you, arise.'*" and Mark 15:34,

---

[27] Aramaic is a Semitic language which gradually supplanted Akkadian as the common tongue of the Near East in the 7th and 6th centuries BC. It later became the official language of the Persian Empire. Aramaic replaced Hebrew as the language of the Jews; portions of the Old Testament books of Daniel and Ezra are written in Aramaic, as are the Babylonian and Jerusalem Talmuds. Its period of greatest influence extended from 300 BC until 650 CE, after which it was gradually supplanted by Arabic. (*The New Encyclopaedia Britannica*, vol. 1, p. 516)

"And at the ninth hour, Jesus cried with a loud voice, 'E'lo-i, E'lo-i, la'ma sabachtha'ni?' which means, 'My God, my God, why hast thou forsaken me?'" [28]

The New Testament Gospel of Mark, though considered by Church scholars to be the oldest of the Gospels, was not written by a disciple of Jesus. Biblical scholars concluded, based on the evidence contained in the Gospel, that Mark himself was not a disciple of Jesus. Furthermore, according to them, it is not even certain who Mark really was. The ancient Christian author, Eusebius (325 C.E.), reported that another ancient author, Papias (130 C.E.), was the first to attribute the Gospel to John Mark, a companion of Paul. [29] Others suggested that he may have been the scribe of Peter and yet others hold that he was probably someone else.

The same is the case with the other Gospels. Although Matthew, Luke and John are the names of disciples of Jesus, the authors of the Gospels bearing their names were not those famous disciples; but other individuals who used the disciples' names to give their accounts credibility. In fact, all the Gospels originally circulated anonymously. Authoritative names were later assigned to them by unknown figures in the early church. [30]

---

[28] *Encyclopedia Americana*, vol. 3, p. 654.

[29] The Five Gospels, p. 20, and *The New Encyclopaedia Britannica*, vol. 14, p. 824. For references to various Marks in the *New Testament*, see the following: Acts 12:12, 25; 13:5; 15:36-41; Colossians 4:10; 2 Timothy 4:11; Philemon 24; and I Peter 5:13.

[30] *The Five Gospels*, p. 20.

Books	Authors
Gospel of Matthew	Unknown[31]
Gospel of Mark	Unknown[32]
Gospel of Luke	Unknown[33]
Gospel of John	Unknown[34]
Acts	The author of Luke[35]
I, II, III John	The author of John[36]

J.B. Phillips, a prebendary[37] of the Chichester Cathedral, the Anglican Church of England, wrote the following preface for his translation of the Gospel according to St. Matthew: "Early tradition ascribed this Gospel to the apostle Matthew, but scholars nowadays almost all reject this view. The author, whom we can conveniently call Matthew, has plainly drawn on the mysterious

---

[31] Although there is a Matthew named among the various lists of Jesus' disciples...the writer of Matthew is probably anonymous." *The New Encyclopaedia Britannica*, vol. 14, p. 826.

[32] "Though the author of Mark is probably unknown..." *The New Encyclopaedia Britannica*, vol. 14, p. 824.

[33] The Muratorian Canon refers to Luke, the physician, Paul's companion; Irenaeus depicts Luke as a follower of Paul's gospel. Eusebius has Luke as an Antiochene physician who was with Paul in order to give the Gospel apostolic authority." *The New Encyclopaedia Britannica*, vol. 14, p. 827.

[34] "From internal evidence the Gospel was written by a beloved disciple whose name is unknown." *The New Encyclopaedia Britannica*, vol. 14, p. 828.

[35] *The New Encyclopaedia Britannica*, vol. 14, p. 830.

[36] Ibid., vol. 14, p. 844.

[37] A priest who receives income from the revenue of a church, especially a cathedral. (*Oxford Advanced Learner's Dictionary*, p. 973.)

"*Q*",[38] which may have been a collection of oral traditions. He has used Mark's Gospel freely, though he has rearranged the order of events and has in several instances used different words for what is plainly the same story."[39] The Fourth Gospel (John) was opposed as heretical in the early church, and it knows none of the stories associated with John, son of Zebedī.[40] In the judgement of many scholars, it was produced by a "school" of disciples, probably in Syria in the last decade of the first century.[41]

---

[38] There are about two hundred identical verses found in both Matthew and Luke (e.g. Matt 3:7-10 & Luke 3:7-9; Matt. 18:10-14 & Luke 15:3-7), with no equivalent in either Mark or John. As a way of explaining this striking agreement, a German scholar hypothesized that there once existed a source document, which he referred to as a *Quelle* (German for "source"). The abbreviation "*Q*" was later adopted as its name.

The existence of *Q* was once challenged by some scholars on the grounds that a sayings-gospel was not really a gospel. The challengers argued that there were no ancient parallels to a gospel containing only sayings and parables and lacking stories about Jesus, especially the story about his trial and death. The discovery of the Gospel of Thomas changed all that. (*The Five Gospels*, p. 12.) Thomas contains one hundred and fourteen sayings and parables ascribed to Jesus; it has no narrative framework: no account of Jesus' exorcisms, healings, trial, death, and resurrection; no birth or childhood stories; and no narrated account of his public ministry in Galilee and Judea. The Coptic translation of this document (written about 350 C.E.), found in 1945 at Nag Hammadi in Egypt, has enabled scholars to identify three Greek fragments (dated around 200 C.E.), discovered earlier, as pieces of three different copies of the same gospel. Thomas has forty-seven parallels to Mark, forty parallels to *Q*, seventeen to Matthew, four to Luke, and five to John. About sixty-five sayings or parts of sayings are unique to Thomas. (*The Five Gospels*, p.15).

[39] *The Gospels in Modern English.*

[40] Since the late 18th century, the first three Gospels have been called the Synoptic Gospels, because the texts, set side by side, show a similar treatment of the life and death of Jesus Christ. (*The New Encyclopaedia Britannica*, vol. 5, p. 379).

[41] *The Five Gospels*, p. 20.

Contradictions

Evidence for the unreliability of much of the material in the Bible can also be found in the many contradictions in the texts of the Old and New Testaments. The following are only a few examples:

The Old Testament

1) The authors of Samuel and Chronicles relate the same story about Prophet David taking a census of the Jews. However, in 2nd Samuel, it states that Prophet David acted on **God's** instructions, while in 1st Chronicles, he acted on **Satan's** instructions.

II SAMUEL 24	I CHRONICLES 21
The Numbering	*The Numbering*
And again the anger of the Lord was kindled against Israel, and he moved David against them to say, "Go, number Israel and Judah."	And <u>Satan</u> stood up against Israel, and provoked David to number Israel.

2) In describing the length of a plague prophesied by Gad [42], the author of 2nd Samuel listed it as **seven** years, while the author of 1st Chronicles listed it as **three** years.

---

[42] And the Lord spoke to Gad, David's seer, saying," I Chronicles, 21:91. According to this text, Gad was the name of Prophet David's personal fortune teller.

II SAMUEL 24:13
The Plague
So Gad came to David and told him, and said unto him, "Shall seven years of famine come unto thee in thy land? or wilt thou flee three months before thine enemies, while they pursue thee?"

I CHRONICLES 21:11
The Plague 11
So Gad came to David, and said unto him, "Thus saith the Lord, 'Choose thee 12 Either three years' famine; or three months to be destroyed before thy foes, while that the sword of thine enemies overtaketh thee;' "

3) In 2nd Chronicles, Jehoiachin was described as being **eight** years old when he began to reign, while in 2nd Kings he is described as being **eighteen** years old.

II CHRONICLES 36:9
The Age
Jehoiachin was eight years old when he began to reign, and he reigned three months and ten days in Jerusalem: and he did that which was evil in the sight of the Lord.

II KINGS 24:8
The Age
Jehoiachin was eighteen years old when he began to reign, and he reigned in Jerusalem three months. And his mother's name was Nehushta, the daughter of Elnathan of Jerusalem.

4) The author of 2nd Samuel described the number of Syrians who died during a battle with Prophet David as being **seven hundred**, while the author of 1st Chronicles gave their number as **seven thousand**.

II SAMUEL 10:18	I CHRONICLES 19:18
The Dead	*The Dead*
And the Syrians fled before Israel; and David slew the men of <u>seven hundred</u> chariots of the Syrians, and forty thousand <u>horsemen</u>, and smote Shobach the captain of their host, who died there.	But the Syrians fled before Israel; and David slew of the Syrians <u>seven thousand</u> men which fought in chariots, and forty thousand <u>footmen</u>, and killed Shophach the captain of the host.

Although some may say that the adding or dropping of a '1' or a zero is not significant, as it is only a copying mistake, here that is not the case because the Jews spelled out their numbers in words and did not use numerals.

Such discrepancies cannot be accepted as part of a divinely revealed text. Moreover, they prove the fallibility of the human authors and further prove that the texts of the Old Testament were not divinely preserved.

The New Testament

In the New Testament many similar contradictions may also be found. The following are but a few:

1) The Gospel accounts vary regarding who carried the cross on which Jesus was supposed to have been crucified. In Matthew, Mark and Luke, it was Simon of Cyrene, and in John, it was Jesus.

LUKE, 23:26[43]

The Cross

As they led him away, they seized a man, <u>Simon of Cyrene</u>, who was coming from the country, and <u>they laid the cross on him and made him carry it</u>...

JOHN, 19:16

The Cross

Then he (Pilate) handed him over to them to be crucified. So <u>they took Jesus; and carrying the cross himself</u>, he went to what is called the Place of the Skull,...

2) After Jesus' "crucifixion", the Gospel accounts differ as to who visited his tomb, when the visit took place, as well as the state of the tomb when it was visited. The Gospels of Matthew, Luke and John state that the visit took place **before sunrise**, while the Gospel of Mark states that it was **after sunrise**. In another three Gospels (Mark, Luke and John) the women found the stone door of the tomb rolled away, but in one (Matthew) the tomb was closed until an angel descended before them and rolled it away.

MARK, 16:1-2

The Visit

And when the sabbath was past, Mary Magdalene, and Mary the Mother of James, and Salome, bought spices, so that they might go and anoint him. [2]And very early on the first day of the week they went to the tomb <u>when the sun had risen.</u>

JOHN, 20:1[44]

The Visit

Now on the first day of the week Mary Magdalene came to the tomb early, <u>while it was still dark</u>, and saw that the stone had been taken away from the tomb.

---

[43] See also, Matthew 27:32 and Mark 15:21.

[44] See also, Luke 24:1-2.

MATTHEW, 28:1-2
The Visit
Now after the sabbath, <u>toward</u>
<u>the dawn</u> of the first day of the
week, Mary Magdalene and the
other Mary went to see the
sepulchre. **2** And behold, there
was a great earthquake; for an
angel of the Lord descended
from heaven and came and
rolled back the stone, and sat
upon it.

3) The New Testament accounts vary regarding the fate of Judas
Iscariot and the money he received for betraying Jesus. In
Matthew, he hung himself, while in Acts, he fell in a field
and died there.

MATTHEW, 27:3-6
The Fate of Judas
When Judas, his betrayer, saw
that Jesus was condemned, he
repented and brought back the
thirty pieces of silver to the
chief priests and the elders,...
And throwing down the pieces
of silver in the temple, he
departed; and <u>he went and</u>
<u>hanged himself</u>.

ACTS, 1:18
The Fate of Judas
Now this man acquired a
field with the reward of his
wickedness; and falling
headlong, <u>he burst open in</u>
<u>the middle and all his bowels</u>
<u>gushed out</u>.

4) When the genealogy of Jesus from David in Matthew 1:6-16, is compared to that of Luke 3:23-31, there are major discrepancies. Firstly, Jesus in Matthew has 26 parents between himself and David, but in Luke he has 41. Secondly, the names in both lists vary radically after David, and only two names are the same: Joseph, and Zorobabel. Both lists start off with Joseph, strangely enough, as the father of Jesus, but in Matthew, the author records Jesus' paternal grandfather as being **Jacob**, while in Luke he is **Heli**. If one were to accept the suggestion of some that one of the lists is actually the genealogy of Mary, it could not possibly account for any differences after their common ancestor David. Both lists meet again at Abraham and between David and Abraham most of the names are the same. However, in Matthew's list, Hezron's son's name is **Ram**, the father of Ammin'adab, while in Luke's list, Hezron's son's name is **Arni**, whose son's name is **Admin**, the father of Ammin'adab.[45] Consequently, between David and Abraham there are 12 forefathers in Matthew's list and 13 in Luke's list.

These discrepancies and many others like them in the Gospels are clearly errors that cast a shadow of doubt on their authenticity as divinely revealed texts. Consequently, most Christian scholars today look at the Old and New Testament books as human accounts which they believe were inspired by God. However, even the claim that they were inspired by God is questionable as it implies that God inspired the authors to write mistakes and contradictions in His scriptures.

Having established that the authenticity of both the New and the Old Testament is questionable, it can then be said with

---

[45] Also in Matthew's list, Nahshon's son's name is **Salmon**, while in Luke's list, Nahshon's son's name is **Sala**.

certainty that the Bible cannot be used by itself as an authentic reference source for establishing who Jesus was, nor the content of his message.

The Qur'an

On the other hand, the Qur'an — believed by Muslims to be the word of God revealed to Prophet Muhammad (ﷺ) — was written down and memorized, from beginning to end, during the lifetime of the Prophet himself.

Within a year after his death, the first standard written text was produced.[46] And within 14 years after his death, authorized copies (the 'Uthmanic recension) made from the standard codex[47] were sent to the capitals of the Muslim state, and unauthorized copies were destroyed.[48]

Since the Prophet's death in 632 CE, an increasing number of people in each successive generation have memorized the complete text of the Qur'an from beginning to end. Today there exist tens of thousands of people around the world who recite the whole text, from memory, during the month of Ramaḍân every year, as well as on other occasions.

One of the leading orientalists, Kenneth Cragg, said the following regarding the memorization and preservation of the Qur'anic text, "This phenomenon of Qur'anic recital means that the text has traversed the centuries in an unbroken living sequence

---

[46] *Shorter Encyclopaedia of Islam*, p. 278.

[47] A handwritten book of ancient texts (*pl* codices).

[48] *Shorter Encyclopaedia of Islam*, p. 279. See also *The New Encyclopaedia Britannica*, vol. 22, p. 8.

of devotion. It cannot, therefore, be handled as an antiquarian thing, nor as a historical document out of a distant past."[49] Another orientalist scholar, William Graham, wrote: "For countless millions of Muslims over more than fourteen centuries of Islamic history, 'scripture', *al-kitâb* has been a book learned, read and passed on by vocal repetition and memorisation. The written Qur'an may 'fix' visibly the authoritative text of the Divine Word in a way unknown in history, but the authoritativeness of the Qur'anic book is only realised in its fullness and perfection when it is correctly recited."[50] Yet another, John Burton, stated: "The method of transmitting the Qur'an from one generation to the next, by having the young memorise the oral tradition of their elders, had mitigated somewhat from the beginning the worst perils of relying solely on written records..."[51] At the end of a voluminous work on the Qur'an's collection, Burton stated that the text of the Qur'an available today is "the text which has come down to us in the form which was organised and approved by the Prophet... What we have today in our hands is the *muṣ-ḥaf*[52] of Muhammad."[53]

Scriptual Criticism

The same principles of analysis which were applied to Bible manuscripts by Bible scholars and which exposed the flaws and changes, have been applied to Qur'anic manuscripts gathered from around the world. Ancient manuscripts found in the Library

---

[49] *The Mind of the Qur'an*, p. 26.

[50] *Beyond the Written Word*, p. 80.

[51] *An Introduction to the Hadith*, p. 27.

[52] The Arabic term used to refer to the text of the Qur'an.

[53] *The Collection of the Qur'an*, Pp. 239-40.

of Congress in Washington, the Chester Beatty Museum in Dublin, Ireland, the London Museum, as well as Museums in Tashkent, Turkey and Egypt, from all periods of Islamic history, have been compared. The result of all such studies confirm that there has not been any change in the text from its original writing. For example, the *"Institute fur Koranforschung"* of the University of Munich, Germany, collected and collated over 42,000 complete or incomplete copies of the Qur'an. After some fifty years of study, they reported that in terms of differences among the various copies, there were no variants, except occasional mistakes of copyists, which could easily be ascertained. The institute was destroyed by American bombs during the Second World War.[54]

Contradictions in the Qur'an

The Qur'an remains in its original language, Arabic, and the Qur'an challenges its readers in Chapter *an-Nisâ*, (4):82, to find any errors in it, if they do not believe it is really from God.

﴿أَفَلَا يَتَدَبَّرُونَ ٱلْقُرْءَانَ وَلَوْ كَانَ مِنْ عِندِ غَيْرِ ٱللَّهِ لَوَجَدُواْ فِيهِ ٱخْتِلَٰفًا كَثِيرًا ۝﴾

(سورة النِّساء: ٨٢)

◆Will they not consider the Qur'an carefully? Had it been from other than Allah, they would have found many contradictions in it.◆
(Qur'an 4: 82)

The few "apparent contradictions" commonly mentioned by those who attempt to reduce the Qur'an to the level of the Bible are easily explained. For example, the "first believer" in the following two verses:

---

[54] *Muhammad Rasoolullâh*, p. 179.

Chapter *al-An'âm* **(6):14**
❨Say [O' Muhammad]: 'Shall I adopt as my lord someone other than Allah, Creator of the heavens and earth, though it is He Who feeds but is not fed?' Say: 'Indeed I am commanded to be the first of those who submit themselves [to Allah], and not to be among the idolaters.'❩

Chapter *al-A'râf* **(7):143**
❨...But when his Lord appeared to the mountain, it crumbled to dust, and Moses fell down unconscious. When he regained consciousness, he said, 'Glory be to You, I turn to you in repentance and I am the first of the believers.'❩

The earlier verse refers to Prophet Muhammad, who was told to inform the pagans of his time that he could never accept their idolatry and would be the first of those in his time to submit to Allah. In the second verse, Prophet Moses declares himself among the first in his time to submit to Allah upon realizing that it was impossible to see Allah. Each prophet was the first in his own era to submit to Allah.

Similarly, the "day with God" mentioned in the following two verses:

Chapter *as-Sajdah* **(32):5**
❨He arranges [every] affair from the heavens to the earth, then it goes up to Him, in a day equivalent to a thousand years according to your reckoning.❩

Chapter *al-Mi'râj* **(70):4**
❨The angels and the Spirit ascend to Him in a day equivalent to fifty thousand years.❩

The two verses refer to two completely different events. The first refers to the destiny that is sent down and reported back in a day governing a thousand years of human life.[55] The second refers to the ascent of the angels from the world to the highest of the heavens, which for them takes a day equivalent to 50,000 human years.[56] Allah is not governed by time. He created time and made it relative to the creatures it governs. Consequently, according to the calculation of modern scientists, one year on Mars is equivalent to 687 earth days, while one year on Uranus is equal to 84 earth years.[57]

The Qur'anic text is remarkably consistent in its thought and presentation. In the preface of one of the best orientalist translations of the Qur'an, the translator, Arthur John Arberry, writes: "There is a repertory of familiar themes running through the whole Koran; each *Soorah*[58] elaborates or adumbrates[59] one or more — often many — of these. Using the language of music, each *Soorah* is a rhapsody composed of whole or fragmentary *leitmotivs*;[60] the analogy is reinforced by the subtly varied rhythmical flow of the discourse."[61]

Scientific references in the Qur'anic text have proven to be consistently and explicitly accurate. In a lecture given at the French Academy of Medicine, in 1976, entitled "Physiological and Embryological Data in the Qur'an", Dr. Maurice Bucaille said, "There is no human work in existence that contains statements as far beyond the level of knowledge of its time as the

---

[55] *Tafseer al-Qurṭubi*, vol. 8, Pp. 5169-70.

[56] *Fat-ḥul-Qadeer*, vol. 4, p. 349.

[57] *The New Encyclopaedia Britannica*, vol. 27, Pp. 551 & 571.

[58] Qur'anic chapter.

[59] Indicate faintly or in outline.

[60] Recurring features.

[61] *The Koran Interpreted*, p. 28.

Qur'an. Scientific opinions comparable to those in the Qur'an are the result of modern knowledge."[62]

Speaking about the authority of the Qur'an, Professor Reynold A. Nicholson said, "We have (in the Koran) materials of unique and incontestable authority for tracing the origin and early development of Islam, such materials as do not exist in the case of Buddhism or Christianity or any other ancient religion."[63]

Consequently, it is only the Qur'an that represents an accurate means of determining who Jesus was and what his message was. Moreover, the Qur'an can also be used to determine to what degree some of the revealed word of God exists within the Bible.

In the Qur'an, God commands the believers to accept, as a part of their faith, the divine word revealed to Prophet Moses, known as the Torah; to Prophet David in the original Psalms; and to Jesus in the original Gospel. All Muslims are obliged to believe in all of the revealed scriptures. However, as stated in the Qur'an, all scriptures revealed before the Qur'an have not remained as they were revealed. People changed parts of them to suit their own desires.

﴿فَوَيْلٌ لِّلَّذِينَ يَكْتُبُونَ ٱلْكِتَٰبَ بِأَيْدِيهِمْ ثُمَّ يَقُولُونَ هَٰذَا مِنْ عِندِ ٱللَّهِ لِيَشْتَرُواْ بِهِۦ ثَمَنًا قَلِيلًا فَوَيْلٌ لَّهُم مِّمَّا كَتَبَتْ أَيْدِيهِمْ وَوَيْلٌ لَّهُم مِّمَّا يَكْسِبُونَ ٧٩﴾

(سورة البَقَرَة: ٧٩)

❨Woe to those who write the scripture with their own hands and then say: 'This is from Allah,' to purchase with it [worldly gain] at a cheap price. Woe to them for what their hands have written and

---

[62] *The Qur'an and Modern Science*, p. 6.

[63] *Literary History of the Arabs*, p. 143.

woe to them for what they earned by doing it.❫ *(Qur'an 2: 79)*

Furthermore, in the Old Testament, God is quoted in Jeremiah 8:8 as saying, *"How can you say, 'We are wise, and the law is with us?' But, behold, the false pen of the scribes has made it into a lie."*[64]

❬Woe to those who write the scripture with their own hands and then say, "This is from Allah," to purchase with it [worldly gain] at a cheap price. Woe to them for what their hands have written and

---

[64] *Revised Standard Version.*

CHAPTER TWO

JESUS, THE PERSON

$\mathcal{A}$s has been shown in the previous chapter, the Biblical scriptures, both New and Old Testaments, are unreliable sources and cannot, therefore, be used as an authentic means of knowing the truth about the man called Jesus Christ or about his mission and message. However, a close examination of these scriptures in the light of Qur'anic verses will reveal some of the truths about Jesus that have survived in the Bible.

A Messenger

Throughout the Qur'an, Jesus is identified fundamentally as a Messenger of God. In Chapter *aṣ-Ṣaff*, (61):6, God quotes Jesus as follows:

﴿وَإِذْ قَالَ عِيسَى ٱبْنُ مَرْيَمَ يَٰبَنِىٓ إِسْرَٰٓءِيلَ إِنِّى رَسُولُ ٱللَّهِ إِلَيْكُم مُّصَدِّقًا لِّمَا بَيْنَ يَدَىَّ مِنَ ٱلتَّوْرَىٰةِ﴾

(سورة الصّف: ٦)

﴿And [remember] when Jesus, son of Mary, said: 'O Children of Israel, I am the messenger of Allah sent to you, confirming the Torah [which came] before me.﴾   *(Qur'an 61: 6)*

There are many verses in the New Testament supporting the

messengership / prophethood of Jesus. The following are only a few: In Matthew 21:11, the people of his time are recorded as referring to Jesus as a prophet: "*And the crowds said, 'This is the prophet Jesus of Nazareth of Galilee.'*" In Mark, 6:4, it is stated that Jesus referred to himself as a prophet: "*And Jesus said to them, 'A prophet is not without honour, except in his own country, and among his own kin, and in his own house.'*" In the following verses, Jesus is referred to as having been sent as a messenger is sent. In Matthew 10:40, Jesus was purported to have said: "*He that receiveth you receiveth me, and he that receiveth me receiveth him that sent me.*" In John 17:3, Jesus is also quoted as saying: "*And this is life eternal, that they might know thee the only true God, and Jesus Christ, whom thou hast sent.*"[1]

A Man

The Qur'anic revelation not only affirms Jesus' prophethood, but it also clearly denies Jesus' divinity. In Chapter *al-Mâ'idah*, (5): 75, God points out that Jesus ate food, which is a human act, obviously not befitting to God.

﴿مَّا ٱلْمَسِيحُ ٱبْنُ مَرْيَمَ إِلَّا رَسُولٌ قَدْ خَلَتْ مِن قَبْلِهِ ٱلرُّسُلُ وَأُمُّهُ صِدِّيقَةٌ كَانَا يَأْكُلَانِ ٱلطَّعَامَ ٱنظُرْ كَيْفَ نُبَيِّنُ لَهُمُ ٱلْآيَتِ ثُمَّ ٱنظُرْ أَنَّىٰ يُؤْفَكُونَ ٧٥﴾

(سورة المائدة: ٧٥)

❨The Messiah, Son of Mary, was no more than a messenger and many messengers passed away before him. His mother was exceedingly truthful, and they both ate food. See how I have made the signs clear for them, yet see how they are deluded.❩

(Qur'an 5: 75)

---

[1] See also, John 4:34, 5:30, 7:16 & 28, 11:42, 13:16, 14:24.

There are numerous accounts in the New Testament which also deny Jesus' divinity.

For example, in Matthew 19:17, Jesus responded to one who addressed him as "O good master", saying: "*Why callest thou me good? There is none good but one, that is God.*" If he rejected being called "good",[2] and stated that only God is truly good, he clearly implies that he is not God.

In John 14:28, Jesus is quoted as saying: "*The Father is greater than I.*" By stating that the "Father" is greater than himself, Jesus distinguishes himself from God. Also in John 20:17, Jesus told Mary Magdalene to tell his followers: "*I ascend unto my Father and your Father; and to my God and your God.*" Jesus' reference to God as "my Father and your Father" further emphasizes the distinction between himself and God. Furthermore, by referring to God as "his God", he left no room for anyone to intelligently claim that he was God.

Even in some of the writings of Paul, which the Church has taken to be sacred, Jesus is referred to as a "man", distinct and different from God. In 1st Timothy, 2:5, Paul writes: "*For there is one God, and one mediator between God and men, the man Christ Jesus.*"

There are also verses in the Qur'an which confirm Prophet Muhammad's humanity, in order to prevent his followers from elevating him to a divine or semi-divine status, as was done to Prophet Jesus. For example, in Chapter *al-Kahf*, (18):110, Allah instructs Prophet Muhammad (ﷺ) to inform all who hear his message:

---

[2] Jesus here rejects being called 'perfectly good', because perfection belongs only to God. He was 'good', but, being the "Son of man" (Mat. 19:29)—as he liked to call himself—he was capable of error.

﴾قُل إِنَّمَآ أَنَا۟ بَشَرٌ مِّثْلُكُمْ يُوحَىٰٓ إِلَىَّ أَنَّمَآ إِلَٰهُكُمْ إِلَٰهٌ وَٰحِدٌ﴾   (سورة الكهف: ١١٠)

﴿Say: 'Indeed, I am only a man like you to whom it has been revealed that your God is only one God.'﴾   *(Qur'an 18: 110)*

In Chapter *al-A'râf*, (7):187, Allah also directed Prophet Muhammad (ﷺ) to acknowledge that the time of the Judgement is known only to God.

﴿يَسْـَٔلُونَكَ عَنِ ٱلسَّاعَةِ أَيَّانَ مُرْسَىٰهَا قُلْ إِنَّمَا عِلْمُهَا عِندَ رَبِّى لَا يُجَلِّيهَا لِوَقْتِهَآ إِلَّا هُوَ﴾
(سورة الأعراف: ١٨٧)

﴿They ask you about the Final Hour: 'When will its appointed time be?' Say: 'Knowledge of it is with my Lord. None can reveal its time except Him.'﴾   *(Qur'an 7: 187)*

In the Gospel according to Mark, 13:31-32, Jesus is also reported to have denied having knowledge of when the final hour of this world would be, saying: "*Heaven and the earth shall pass away but my word shall not pass away, but of that day or hour no man knoweth, neither the angels in the heaven nor the Son but the Father.*" One of the attributes of God is omniscience, knowledge of all things. Therefore, his denial of knowledge of the Day of Judgement is also a denial of divinity, for one who does not know the time of the final hour cannot possibly be God.[3]

An Immaculate Conception

The Qur'an confirms the Biblical story of Jesus' virgin birth. However, in the Qur'anic account of Jesus' birth, Mary was an

---

[3] It should be noted that, in spite of the Qur'anic warnings and other statements of Prophet Muhammad himself, few Muslims have elevated him to semi-divine status by directing their prayers to or through him.

unmarried maiden whose life was dedicated to the worship of God by her mother. While she was worshipping in a place of religious seclusion, angels came and informed her of her impending pregnancy.

$$\text{﴿إِذْ قَالَتِ ٱلْمَلَٰئِكَةُ يَٰمَرْيَمُ إِنَّ ٱللَّهَ يُبَشِّرُكِ بِكَلِمَةٍ مِّنْهُ ٱسْمُهُ ٱلْمَسِيحُ عِيسَى ٱبْنُ مَرْيَمَ وَجِيهًا فِى ٱلدُّنْيَا وَٱلْءَاخِرَةِ وَمِنَ ٱلْمُقَرَّبِينَ ﴾}$$

(سورة آل عِمرَان: ٤٥)

❨When the angels said: 'O Mary, indeed Allah gives you glad tidings of a Word from Him, whose name will be the Messiah, Jesus the son of Mary. He will be honoured in this world and the next and will be of those close to Allah.'❩   *(Qur'an 3: 45)*

$$\text{﴿قَالَتْ رَبِّ أَنَّىٰ يَكُونُ لِى وَلَدٌ وَلَمْ يَمْسَسْنِى بَشَرٌ قَالَ كَذَٰلِكِ ٱللَّهُ يَخْلُقُ مَا يَشَآءُ إِذَا قَضَىٰ أَمْرًا فَإِنَّمَا يَقُولُ لَهُ كُن فَيَكُونُ ﴾}$$

(سورة آل عِمرَان: ٤٧)

❨She said: 'O my Lord, how can I have a son when no man has touched me?' He said: 'Even so — Allah creates what He wishes. When He decrees something, He only has to say to it: "Be!" and it is.'❩   *(Qur'an 3: 47)*

However, the Qur'an clarifies that Jesus' virgin birth did not change the state of his humanity. His creation was like the creation of Adam, who had neither father nor mother.

$$\text{﴿إِنَّ مَثَلَ عِيسَىٰ عِندَ ٱللَّهِ كَمَثَلِ ءَادَمَ خَلَقَهُ مِن تُرَابٍ ثُمَّ قَالَ لَهُ كُن فَيَكُونُ ﴾}$$

(سورة آل عِمرَان: ٥٩)

❨Surely, the example of Jesus, in Allah's sight, is like that of Adam. He created him from dust and said: 'Be!' and he was.❩

(Qur'an 3: 59)

The Miracles

The Qur'anic account of Jesus' ministry confirms most [4] of his miracles mentioned in the Bible and identifies some not mentioned in the Bible. For example, the Qur'an informs that Jesus was a messenger of God from his birth, and his first miracle was speaking as a child in the cradle. After Mary had given birth to Jesus, people accused her of fornication. Instead of responding to their accusations, she pointed to her newly born child:

﴿فَأَشَارَتْ إِلَيْهِ قَالُوا كَيْفَ نُكَلِّمُ مَن كَانَ فِي ٱلْمَهْدِ صَبِيًّا ۝ قَالَ إِنِّي عَبْدُ ٱللَّهِ ءَاتَىٰنِيَ ٱلْكِتَٰبَ وَجَعَلَنِي نَبِيًّا ۝﴾ (سورة مَرْيَم: ٢٩-٣٠)

﴾[When] she pointed to him, they asked, 'How can we talk to a child in the cradle?' He [Jesus] said: 'Indeed, I am a servant of Allah. He gave me the scripture and made me a prophet.'﴿

(Qur'an 19: 29-30)

Among his other miracles of bringing the dead back to life, healing lepers, and making the blind see, the Qur'an records another miracle not mentioned in the Bible. Prophet Jesus fashioned birds out of clay, blew on them and they flew away, living birds. But the point which is emphasized throughout the Qur'an is that whenever Jesus performed a miracle, he informed the people that it was by God's permission. He made it clear to his followers that he was not doing the miracles by himself, in the same way that the earlier Prophets made it clear to those around them.

Unfortunately, those who claim divinity for Jesus, usually hold up his miracles as evidence. However, other prophets were

---

[4] The Biblical story of Jesus turning water into wine (John 2:1-10) is conspicuously absent from the Qur'an.

recorded to have done the same or similar miracles in the Old
Testament.

Jesus fed 5,000 people with five loaves of bread and two fishes.	Elisha fed 100 people with twenty barley loaves and a few ears of corn. (II Kings 4:44)
Jesus healed lepers.	Elisha cured Naaman the leper. (II Kings 5:14)
Jesus caused the blind to see.	Elisha caused the blind to see. (II Kings 6:17&20)
Jesus raised the dead.	Elisha did the same. (I Kings 17:22) So did Elisha. (II Kings 4:34) Even Elisha's bones could restore the dead. (II Kings 13:21)
Jesus walked on water.	Moses and his people crossed the dead sea. (Exodus 14:22)

There are also texts in the New Testament which confirm that
Jesus did not act on his own. Jesus is quoted in John 5:30, as
saying: "*I can of mine own self do nothing...*" and in Luke 11:20,
as saying, "*But if I with the finger of God cast out devils, no doubt
the Kingdom of God is come upon you.*" In Acts 2:22, Paul writes:
"*Men of Israel, hear these words: Jesus of Nazareth, a man
attested to you by God with mighty works and wonders and signs
which God did through him in your midst, as you yourselves
know...*"

"Evidence" for Jesus' Divinity

There is a number of verses which have been interpreted by the Catholic and Protestant Churches as evidence for the Divinity of Jesus Christ. However, on close examination of these verses, it becomes evident that, either their wordings are ambiguous, leaving them open to a number of different interpretations, or they are additions not found in the early manuscripts of the Bible. The following are some of the most commonly quoted arguments.

1. The alpha and omega

In the Book of Revelation 1, verse 8, it is implied that Jesus said the following about himself: *"I am Alpha and Omega, the beginning and the ending, saith the Lord, which is, and which was, and which is to come, the Almighty."* These are the attributes of God. Consequently, Jesus, according to early Christians, is here claiming divinity. However, the above-mentioned wording is according to the *King James Version*. In the *Revised Standard Version,* biblical scholars corrected the translation and wrote : *"I am the Alpha and the Omega," says* **the Lord God***, who is and who was and who is to come, the Almighty."* A correction was also made in the *New American Bible* produced by Catholics. The translation of that verse has been amended to put it in its correct context as follows: *"**The Lord God** says: 'I am the Alpha and the Omega, the one who is and who was, and who is to come, the Almighty.' "* With these corrections, it becomes evident that this was a statement of God and not a statement of Prophet Jesus.

2. The pre-existence of Christ

Another verse commonly used to support the divinity of Jesus is John 8:58: *"Jesus said unto them, 'Verily, verily, I say unto you, Before Abraham was, I am.'"* This verse is taken to imply that Jesus existed prior to his appearance on earth. The conclusion drawn from it is that Jesus must be God, since his existence predates his birth on earth. However, the concept of the preexistence of the prophets, and of man in general, exists in both the Old Testament, as well as in the Qur'an. Jeremiah described himself in The Book of Jeremiah 1:4-5 as follows: *"**4** Now the word of the Lord came to me saying, **5**' Before I formed you in the womb I knew you, and before you were born I consecrated you; I appointed you a prophet to the nations.'"*

Prophet Solomon is reported in Proverbs 8:23-27, to have said, *"**23** Ages ago I was set up at the first, before the beginning of the earth. **24** When there were no depths I was brought forth, when there were no springs abounding with water, **25** Before the mountains had been shaped, before the hills, I was brought forth; **26** before he had made the earth with its fields, or the first of the dust of the world, **27** When he established the heavens, I was there."*

According to Job 38:4 and 21, God addresses Prophet Job as follows: *"**4** Where were you when I laid the foundation of the earth? Tell me, if you have understanding... **21** You Know, for you were born then, and the number of your days is great!"*

In the Qur'an, Chapter *al-A'râf*, (7):172, God informed that man existed in the spiritual form before the creation of the physical world.

﴿وَإِذْ أَخَذَ رَبُّكَ مِنْ بَنِي ءَادَمَ مِن ظُهُورِهِمْ ذُرِّيَّتَهُمْ وَأَشْهَدَهُمْ عَلَى أَنفُسِهِمْ أَلَسْتُ
بِرَبِّكُمْ قَالُوا بَلَى شَهِدْنَا أَن تَقُولُوا يَوْمَ الْقِيَامَةِ إِنَّا كُنَّا عَنْ هَذَا غَافِلِينَ ﴿١٧٢﴾﴾

(سورة الأعراف: ١٧٢)

﴾When your Lord gathered all of Adam's descendants [before
creation] and made them bear witness for themselves, saying:
'Am I not your Lord?' They all replied: 'Yes indeed, we bear
witness.' [That was] so you could not say on the Day of
Judgement: 'We were unaware of this.'﴾   *(Qur'an 7: 172)*

Consequently, Prophet Jesus' statement, *"Before Abraham
was, I am,"* cannot be used as evidence of his divinity. Within the
context of John 8:54-58, Jesus is purported to have spoken about
God's knowledge of His prophets, which predates the creation of
this world.

3. The son of God

Another of the evidences used for Jesus' divinity is the
application of the title "Son of God" to Jesus. However, there are
numerous places in the Old Testament where this title has been
given to others.

God called Israel (Prophet Jacob) His "son" when He
instructed Prophet Moses to go to Pharaoh in Exodus 4:22-23, "**22**
*And you shall say to Pharaoh, 'Thus says the Lord, '*Israel is my
first-born son,*' **23** and I say to you, 'Let my son go that he may
serve me.' ''*[5]

In 2nd Samuel 8:13-14, God calls Prophet Solomon His son, "**13**

---

[5] See also, Hosea 1:10, of the *King James Version*.

*He [Solomon] shall build a house for my name, and I will establish the throne of his kingdom for ever. **14** I will be his father, and he shall be my son."*

God promises to make Prophet David His son in Psalms 89:26-27, *"**26** He shall cry unto me, 'Thou art my father, my God, and the rock of my salvation,' **27** Also I will make him my first-born, higher than the kings of the earth."*[6]

Angels are referred to as "sons of God" in The Book of Job 1: 6, *"Now there was a day when the sons of God came to present themselves before the Lord, and Satan also came among them."*[7]

In the New Testament, there are many references to "sons of God" other than Jesus. For example, when the author of the Gospel according to Luke listed Jesus' ancestors back to Adam, he wrote: *"The son of Enos, the son of Seth, the son of Adam, the son of God."*[8]

Some claim that what is unique in the case of Jesus, is that he is the *only begotten*[9] Son of God, while the others are merely "sons of God". However, God is recorded as saying to Prophet David, in Psalms 2:7, *"I will tell the decree of the Lord: He said to me, 'You are my son, today I have begotten you.'"*

---

[6] In the *Revised Standard Version*, it states: *"And I will make him the first-born, the highest of the kings of the earth."* See also Jeremiah 31:9, *"...for I am a father to Israel and Ephraim is my first-born."*

[7] See also, Job 2:1 and 38:4-7. Other references to sons of God can also be found in Genesis 6:2, Deuteronomy 14:1 and Hosea 1:10.

[8] Luke 3:38.

[9] The term "begotten" in Old English meant 'to be fathered by' and it was used to distinguish between Jesus, who was supposed to be the literal son of God, from the figurative use of the term 'son' for God's "created sons".

It should also be noted that nowhere in the Gospels does Jesus actually call himself "Son of God".[10] Instead, he is recorded to have repeatedly called himself "Son of man" (e.g. Luke 9:22) innumerable times. And in Luke 4:41, he actually rejected being called "Son of God": "*And demons also came out of many, crying, 'You are the Son of God!' But he rebuked them, and would not allow them to speak, because they knew that he was the Christ.*"

Since the Hebrews believed that God is One, and had neither wife nor children in any literal sense, it is obvious that the expression "son of God" merely meant to them "Servant of God"; one who, because of his faithful service, was close and dear to God, as a son is to a father. Christians who came from a Greek or Roman background, later misused this term. In their heritage, "son of God" signified an incarnation of a god or someone born of a physical union between male and female gods.[11] When the Church cast aside its Hebrew foundations, it adopted the pagan concept of "son of God", which was entirely different from the

---

[10] In the New Testament Book of Acts, there are several outlines of speeches of the early disciples of Jesus, speeches which date from the year 33 CE, almost forty years before the Four Gospels were written. In one of these discourses, Jesus is referred to specifically as *andra apo tou theou*: "a man from God." (Acts 2:22). Not once do these early confessions of faith use the expression *wios tou theou*: "Son of God", but they do speak several times of Jesus as God's servant and prophet (Acts 3:13, 22, 23, 26). The significance of these speeches is that they accurately reflect the original belief and terminology of the disciples, before the belief and terminology were evolved under the influence of Roman religion and Greek philosophy. They reflect a tradition which is older than that used by the Four Gospels, in which Jesus is not invested with godship or divine sonship. (*Bible Studies From a Muslim Perspective*, p. 12).

[11] See Acts 14:11-13. In the city of Lystra (Turkey), Paul and Barnabas preached, and the pagan peoples claimed that they were gods incarnate. They called Barnabas the Roman god Zeus, and Paul the Roman god Hermes.

Hebrew usage.[12]

Consequently, the use of the term "son of God" should only be understood from the Semitic symbolic sense of a "servant of God", and not in the pagan sense of a literal offspring of God. In the four Gospels, Jesus is recorded as saying: *"Blessed are the peace-makers; they will be called sons of God."*[13]

Likewise, Jesus' use of the term *abba*, "dear father", should be understood similarly. There is a dispute among New Testament scholars as to precisely what *abba* meant in Jesus' time and also as to how widely it was in use by other Jewish sects of that era.

James Barr has recently argued forcefully that it did not have the specially intimate sense that has so often been attributed to it, but that it simply meant "father".[14] To think of God as "our heavenly Father" was by no means new, for in the Lord's prayer he is reported to have taught his disciples to address God in this same familiar way.

4. One with God

Those who claim that Jesus was God, hold that he was not a separate god, but one and the same God incarnate. They draw support for this belief from verse 30 of the Gospel according to John, chapter 10, in which Jesus is reported to have said, *"I and the Father are one."* Out of context, this verse does imply Jesus' divinity. However, when the Jews accused him of claiming divinity, based on that statement, *"Jesus answered them, 'Is it not*

---

[12] *Bible Studies from a Muslim Perspective*, p. 15.

[13] Matthew 5:9.

[14] *Journal of Theological Studies*, vol. 39 and *Theology*, vol. 91, no. 741.

written in your law, 'I said, Ye are gods?'[15],"[16] He clarified for them, with a scriptual example well known to them, that he was using the metaphorical language of the prophets which should not be interpreted as ascribing divinity to himself or to other human beings.

Further evidence is drawn from verses ten and eleven of the Gospel according to John, chapter 14, where people asked Jesus to show them the Father, and he was supposed to have said: *"Do you not believe that I am in the Father and the Father in me? The words that I say to you I do not speak on my own authority; but the Father who dwells in me does his works. 11 Believe me that I am in the Father and the Father in me; or else believe me for the sake of the works themselves."*

These phrases would imply Jesus' divinity, if the remainder of the same Gospel is ignored. However, nine verses later, in John 14:20, Jesus is also recorded as saying to his disciples, *"In that day you will know that I am in my Father, and you in me, and I in you."* Thus, if Jesus' statement *"I am in the Father and the Father is in me"* means that he is God, then so were his disciples. This symbolic statement means oneness of purpose and not oneness of essence. The symbolic interpretation is further emphasized in John 17:20-21, wherein Jesus said, *"**20** I do not pray for these only, but also for those who believe in me through their word, **21** that they may all be one; even as thou, Father, art in me, and I in thee, that they also may be in us, so that the world may believe that thou has sent me."*[17]

---

[15] Jesus is quoting Psalms 82:6 "I have said, '*Ye are gods*: and all of you are the children of the Most High.'"

[16] John 10:34.

[17] See also John 17:11.

5. "He accepted worship"

It is argued that since Jesus is reported to have accepted the worship of some of his followers, he must have been God. However, a closer examination of the texts indicate both a case of dubious translation, as well as misinterpretation. The term "worship" can be found in the *King James Version* and *The Revised Standard Version* accounts of the three wise men who came from the east. They were reported in Matthew 2:2, to have said, *"Where is the baby born to be the king of the Jews? We saw his star when it came up in the east, and we have come to worship him."*[18] However, in *The New American Bible* (Catholic Press, 1970), the text reads: *"Where is the newborn king of the Jews? We observed his star at its rising and have come to pay him homage."*

In *The Revised Standard Version,* John 9:37-38,: **"37** *Jesus said to him, 'You have seen him, and it is he who speaks to you.'* **38** *He said, 'Lord, I believe'*; and *he worshipped him."*[19] However, in *The American Bible,* the scholarly translators added a footnote which read:

9:38 This verse, omitted in important MSS [manuscripts], may be an addition for a baptismal liturgy.

This verse is not found in important ancient manuscripts containing this Gospel. It is probably a later addition made by Church scribes for use in baptismal services.

Furthermore, as a renowned authority on the Bible and its original language, George M. Lamsa, explained, "The Aramaic

---

[18] See also, Matthew 2:8.

[19] See also Matthew 28:9, *"And behold, Jesus met them and said, 'Hail!' And they came up and took hold of his feet and worshipped him."*

word *sagad,* worship, also means to bend or to kneel down. Easterners in greeting each other generally bowed the head or bent down.[20]... *'He worshipped him'* does not imply that he worshipped Jesus as one worshipped God. Such an act would have been regarded as sacrilegious and a breach of the First Commandment in the eyes of the Jews, and the man might have been stoned. But he knelt before him in token of homage and gratitude."[21]

The final scripture, the Qur'an, clarifies the issue of worshipping or not worshipping Jesus, by quoting a conversation which will take place between Jesus and God on the Day of Judgement. Allah states in Chapter *al-Mâ'idah,* (5):116-7:

﴿وَقَالَ ٱللَّهُ يَٰعِيسَى ٱبْنَ مَرْيَمَ ءَأَنتَ قُلْتَ لِلنَّاسِ ٱتَّخِذُونِي وَأُمِّيَ إِلَٰهَيْنِ مِن دُونِ ٱللَّهِ ... ۞ مَا قُلْتُ لَهُمْ إِلَّا مَآ أَمَرْتَنِي بِهِۦٓ أَنِ ٱعْبُدُواْ ٱللَّهَ رَبِّي وَرَبَّكُمْ ... ۞﴾

(سورة المَائدة: ١١٦–١١٧)

❨When Allah will say: "O' Jesus, son of Mary, did you tell people: 'Worship me and my mother as two gods instead of Allah?'"... [Jesus will say]: "I only told them what You commanded me to say: 'Worship Allah, my Lord and your Lord...'"❩

(Qur'an 5: 116-117)

6. "In the beginning was the word"

Perhaps the most commonly quoted 'evidence' for Jesus' divinity is John 1:1&14, "1 *In the beginning was the Word, and*

---

[20] See, for example, I Samuel 25:23, "*When Abigail saw David, she made haste, and alighted from the ass, and fell before David on her face, and bowed to the ground.*"

[21] *Gospel Light,* (1936 ed.), p. 353, quoted in *Jesus,* p. 21.

the Word was with God, and the Word was God.... **14** *And the Word
became flesh and dwelt among us, full of grace and truth;..."*
However, these statements were not made by Jesus Christ, nor
were they attributed to him by the author of the Gospel according
to John. Consequently, these verses do not constitute evidence for
Jesus' divinity, especially considering the doubts held by
Christian scholars about the Fourth Gospel. The Bible scholars
who authored *The Five Gospels* said: "The two pictures painted
by John and the synoptic gospels (i.e., the Gospels of Matthew,
Mark & Luke) cannot both be historically accurate.[22]... The words
attributed to Jesus in the Fourth Gospel are the creation of the
evangelist for the most part, and reflect the developed language of
John's Christian community."[23]

---

[22] The Gospel of John differs so radically from the other three Gospels (the
Synoptic Gospels) that its authenticity is in doubt. For example:

The Synoptic Gospels	The Gospel of John
Jesus' public ministry lasts one year	Jesus' public ministry lasts for three years
Jesus' speaks in brief one-liners and parables	Jesus' speaks in lengthy philosophic discourses
Jesus has little to say about himself	Jesus reflects extensively on his mission and his person
Casting out money changers from the temple is the <u>last</u> event of his earthly mission	Casting out money changers from the temple is the <u>first</u> incident of his mission
Jesus defends the causes of the poor and the oppressed	Jesus has little or nothing to say about the poor and oppressed
Jesus is an exorcist	Jesus performs no exorcisms
Jesus is crucified on 15 Nisan	Jesus is crucified on 14 Nisan, the day of the Jewish passover sacrifice

[23] *The Five Gospels*, p.10.

The Greek term used by the anonymous author of the Fourth Gospel for "word" is *logos*[24] In doing so, the author identifies Jesus with the pagan *logos* of Greek philosophy, who was the divine reason implicit in the cosmos, ordering it and giving it form and meaning.[25]

The idea of the *logos* in Greek thought may be traced back at least to the 6th-century-BC philosopher, Heracleitus, who proposed that there was a *logos* in the cosmic process analogous to the reasoning power in man. Later, the Stoics[26] defined the *logos* as an active, rational and spiritual principle that permeated all reality.[27] The Greek-speaking Jewish philosopher, Judaeus Philo of Alexandria (15 BC - 45 CE), taught that the *logos* was the intermediary between God and the cosmos, being both the agent of creation and the agent through which the human mind can comprehend God.[28] The writings of Philo were preserved and cherished by the Church, and provided the inspiration for a sophisticated Christian philosophical theology. He departed from Platonic thought regarding the *logos* (Word) and called it "the first-begotten Son of God".[29]

---

[24] Its plural is *logoi* and it also means "reason" or "plan".

[25] The concept defined by the term *logos* is also found in Indian, Egyptian, and Persian philosophical and theological systems. (*The New Encyclopaedia Britannica*, vol. 7, p. 440).

[26] Stoics were philosophers who followed the teachings of the thinker Zeno of Citicum (4th-3rd century BC).

[27] They called the *logos* providence, nature, god, and the soul of the universe.

[28] According to Philo and the Middle Platonists, philosophers who interpreted in religious terms the teachings of the 4th-century-BC Greek master philosopher Plato, the *logos* was both immanent in the world and at the same time the transcendent divine mind. (*The New Encyclopaedia Britannica*, vol. 7, p. 440).

[29] *The New Encyclopaedia Britannica*, vol. 9, p. 386.

The identification of Jesus with the *logos*, was further developed in the early Church as a result of attempts made by early Christian theologians and apologists to express the Christian faith in terms that would be intelligible to the Hellenistic world. Moreover, it was to impress their hearers with the view that Christianity was superior to, or heir to, all that was best in pagan philosophy. Thus, in their apologies and polemical works, the early Christian Fathers stated that Christ was the preexistent *logos*.[30]

The Greek word for 'God' used in the phrase "*and the Word was with God*," is the definite form *hotheos*, meaning 'The God'. However, in the second phrase "*and the Word was God*", the Greek word used for 'God' is the indefinite form *tontheos*, which means 'a god'.[31] Consequently, John 1:1, should more accurately be translated, "*In the beginning was the Word, and the Word was with God, and the Word was a god.*" Therefore, if the Word was a 'god' in the literal sense, it would mean that there were two Gods and not one. However, in Biblical language, the term 'god' is used metaphorically to indicate power. For example, Paul referred to the devil as "god" in 2nd Corinthians 4:4, "*In their case the god of this world has blinded the minds of the unbelievers, to keep them from seeing the light of the gospel of the glory of Christ, who is the likeness of God.*" And Moses is referred to as "god" in Exodus 7:1, "*And the Lord said unto Moses, 'See, I have made thee a god to Pharaoh; and Aaron thy brother shall be thy prophet.'*"[32]

---

[30] *The New Encyclopaedia Britannica*, vol. 7, p. 440.

[31] *Christ in Islam*, Pp. 40-1.

[32] This is accoding to the King James Version and the Authorized Version. In the Revised Standard Version, the translation of this verse is rendered, "*And the Lord said to Moses, 'See, I make you as God to Pharaoh; and Aaron your brother shall be your prophet.'*"

Ancient Thoughts

There was serious conflict between the Pauline and the Jerusalem interpretations of Jesus and his message. This conflict, after simmering for years, finally led to a complete break, by which the Pauline Christian Church was founded, comprising in effect a new religion, separated from Judaism. On the other hand, the Jerusalem Nazarenes did not sever their links with Judaism, but regarded themselves as essentially practising Jews, loyal to the Torah, who also believed in Jesus, a human Messiah figure.[33]

When the Jewish insurrection was crushed by the Romans and their Temple destroyed in 70 CE, the Jewish Christians were scattered, and their power and influence as the Mother Church and centre of the Jesus movement was ended.[34] The Pauline Christian movement, which up until 66 CE had been struggling to survive against the strong disapproval of Jerusalem, now began to make headway.

The Jerusalem Church, under the leadership of James, originally known as Nazarenes, later came to be known by the derogatory nickname Ebionites (Hebrew *evyonium,* "poor men"), which some Nazarenes adopted with pride as a reminder of Jesus' saying, 'Blessed are the poor'. After the ascendency of Greco-Roman Church, the Nazarenes became despised as heretics, due to their rejection of the doctrines of Paul.[35]

---

[33] *The Myth-maker*, p. 172.

[34] Seventy years later a Christian Church was reconstituted in Jerusalem, after the city had been devastated by the Romans for a second time and rebuilt as a Gentile city called Aelia Capitolina. This new Christian Church had no continuity with the early 'Jerusalem Church' led by James. Its members were Gentiles, as Eusebius testifies, and its doctrines were those of Pauline Christianity. (Eusebius, *Ecclesiastical History*, III. v. 2-3. quoted in *The Myth-maker*, p. 174).

[35] *The Myth-maker*, p. 175.

According to the ancient Church historian, Irenaeus (c. 185), the Ebionites believed in one God, the Creator, taught that Jesus was the Messiah, used only the Gospel according to Matthew, and rejected Paul as an apostate from the Jewish Law.[36]

Ebionites were known to still exist in the 4th century. Some had left Palestine and settled in Transjordan and Syria and were later known to be in Asia Minor, Egypt and Rome.[37]

Monarchianism,[38] a Gentile Christian movement which developed during the 2nd and 3rd centuries continued to represent the "extreme" monotheistic view of the Ebionites. It held that Christ was a man, miraculously conceived, but was only 'Son of God' due to being filled with divine wisdom and power. This view was taught at Rome about the end of the 2nd century by Theodotus, who was excommunicated by Pope Victor, and taught somewhat later by Artemon, who was excommunicated by Pope Zephyrinus. About 260 CE it was again taught by Paul of Samosata[39], the bishop of Antioch in Syria, who openly preached that Jesus was a man through whom God spoke his Word (*Logos*) and he vigorously affirmed the absolute unity of God.

Between 263 CE and 268 CE at least three church councils were held at Antioch to debate Paul's orthodoxy. The third condemned his doctrine and deposed him. However, Paul enjoyed the patronage of Zenobia, queen of Palmyra, to whom Antioch was then subject, and it was not until 272 CE when the emperor Aurelian defeated Zenobia that the actual deposition was carried out.[40]

---

[36] *The New Encyclopaedia Britannica*, vol. 4, p. 344.

[37] *The New Encyclopaedia Britannica*, vol. 4, p. 344.

[38] Also known as Dynamic or Adoptionist Monarchianism.

[39] *The New Encyclopaedia Britannica*, vol. 8, p. 244.

[40] *The New Encyclopaedia Britannica*, vol. 9, p. 208.

In the late third and early fourth centuries, Arius (b. *c.* 250, Libya — d. 336 CE), a presbyter of Alexandria, Egypt, also taught the finite nature of Christ and the absolute oneness of God, which attracted a large following until he was declared a heretic, by the council of Nicaea, in May 325 CE. During the council, he refused to sign the formula of faith stating that Christ was of the same divine nature as God. However, influential support from colleagues in Asia Minor and from Constantia, the emperor Constantine's daughter, succeeded in effecting Arius' return from exile and his readmission into the church.[41] The movement which he was supposed to have begun, but which was in fact an extension of Jerusalem Nazarene/Jewish Christian belief, came to be known as Arianism and constituted the greatest internal threat to the Pauline Christian orthodoxy's belief in Jesus' divinity.

From 337 to 350 CE Constans, sympathetic to the orthodox Christians, was emperor in the West, and Constantius II, sympathetic to the Arians, was Emperor in the East. Arian influence was so great that at a church council held in Antioch (341 CE), an affirmation of faith was issued which omitted the clause that Jesus had the "same divine nature as God". In 350 CE Constantius II became sole ruler of the empire, and under his leadership the Nicene party (orthodox Christians) was largely crushed. After Constantius II's death in 361 CE, the orthodox Christian majority in the West consolidated its position. However, the defence of absolute monotheism and the suppression of orthodox Christian trinitarian beliefs continued in the East under the Arian emperor Valens (364-383 CE). It was not until emperor Theodosius I (379-395 CE) took up the defence of orthodoxy that Arianism was finally crushed. The unitarian beliefs of Arius,

---

[41] *The New Encyclopaedia Britannica*, vol. 1, Pp. 556-7.

however, continued among some of the Germanic tribes up until the end of the 7th century.[42]

Modern Thoughts

Today, there are many modern scholars in Christianity who hold that Jesus Christ was not God. There is a book written in England by a group of seven biblical scholars, including leading Anglican and other theologians and New Testament scholars, called, *The Myth of God Incarnate*. It caused a great uproar in the General Synod of the Church of England, when it was first published in 1977 CE. In the preface, the editor, John Hick, wrote the following: "The writers of this book are convinced that another major theological development is called for in this last part of the twentieth century. The need arises from growing knowledge of Christian origins, and involves a recognition that Jesus was (as he is presented in Acts 2.21) 'a man approved by God' for a special role within the divine purpose, and that the later conception of him as God incarnate, the Second Person of the Holy Trinity living a human life, is a mythological or poetic way of expressing his significance for us."[43]

There is a broad agreement among New Testament scholars that the historical Jesus did not make the claim to deity that later Christian thought was to make for him; he did not understand himself to be God, or God the Son, incarnate (in the flesh).[44] The late Archbishop Michael Ramsey, who was himself a New Testament scholar, wrote that 'Jesus did not claim deity for

---

[42] *The New Encyclopaedia Britannica*, vol. 1, Pp. 549-50.

[43] *The Myth of God Incarnate*, p. ix.

[44] *The Metaphor of God Incarnate*, Pp. 27-8.

himself.'[45] His contemporary, the New Testament scholar C.F.D. Moule, said that, "Any case for a 'high' Christology that depended on the authenticity of the alleged claims of Jesus about himself, especially in the Fourth Gospel, would indeed be precarious."[46]

In a major study of the origins of the doctrine of the incarnation, James Dunn, who affirms orthodox christology, concludes that "there was no real evidence in the earliest Jesus tradition of what could fairly be called a consciousness of divinity."[47] Again, Brian Hebblethwaite, a staunch upholder of the traditional Nicene-Calcedonian Christology, acknowledges that "it is no longer possible to defend the divinity of Jesus by reference to the claims of Jesus."[48] Hebblethwaite and Dunn, and other scholars like them who still believe in Jesus' divinity, argue instead that Jesus did not know he was God incarnate. This only became known after his resurrection.

Most famous among the Church of England bishops, who doubt Jesus' divinity, is the outspoken Reverend Professor David Jenkins, the Bishop of Durham in England, who openly states that Jesus was not God.[49]

The following article, which appeared in *The Daily News* some years ago, clearly indicates the degree to which there are doubts among the clergy regarding Jesus' divinity.

---

[45] *Jesus and the Living Past*, p. 39.

[46] *The Origin of Christology*, p. 136.

[47] *Christology in the Making*, p. 60.

[48] *The Incarnation*, p. 74.

[49] *The Economist, April 1*, 1989, vol. 311, no. 7596, p. 19.

Shock survey of Anglican bishops

LONDON: More than half of England's Anglican bishops say Christians are not obliged to believe that Jesus Christ was God, according to a survey published today.

The poll of 31 of England's 39 bishops shows that many of them think that Christ's miracles, the virgin birth and the resurrection might not have happened exactly as described in the Bible.

Only 11 of the bishops insisted that Christians must regard Christ as both God and man, while 19 said it was sufficient to regard Jesus as "God's supreme agent". One declined to give a definite opinion.

The poll was carried out by London Weekend Television's weekly religion show, Credo.

"DAILY NEWS" 25/6/84

CHAPTER THREE

THE MESSAGE

T he second issue, 'The Message of Jesus', is perhaps the most important point to consider. For, if Jesus was not God incarnate, but a prophet of God, the message which he brought from God is the essence of his mission.

Submission

The foundation of Jesus' message was submission to the will of God, because that is the foundation of the religion which God prescribed for man since the beginning of time. God says in chapter *Âl 'Imrân*, the third chapter of the Qur'an, verse 19.

(سورة آل عِمرَان: ١٩)   ﴿ ...۞﴾ ﴿إِنَّ ٱلدِّينَ عِندَ ٱللَّهِ ٱلْإِسْلَٰمُ﴾

Truly, the religion in the sight of Allah is Islam [submission]...

(Qur'an 3: 19)

In Arabic, submission to God's will is expressed by the word *'Islam'*. In the Gospel according to Matthew 7:22, Jesus is quoted as saying: "*Not everyone who says to me, 'Lord, Lord,' shall enter the kingdom of heaven, but he who does the will of my Father in heaven.*" In this statement, Jesus places emphasis on "*the will of the Father*"; submission of the human will to the will of God. In

John 5:30, it is narrated that Jesus also said: "*I can do nothing on my own authority; as I hear, I judge; and my judgment is just, because I seek not my own will but the will of him who sent me.*"

The Law

The "will of God" is contained in the divinely revealed laws which the prophets taught their followers. Consequently, obedience to divine law is the foundation of worship. The Qur'an affirms the need for obedience to the divinely revealed laws in chapter *al-Mâ'idah*, verse 44.

﴿ إِنَّآ أَنزَلْنَا ٱلتَّوْرَىٰةَ فِيهَا هُدًى وَنُورٌ يَحْكُمُ بِهَا ٱلنَّبِيُّونَ ٱلَّذِينَ أَسْلَمُواْ ...

وَمَن لَّمْ يَحْكُم بِمَآ أَنزَلَ ٱللَّهُ فَأُوْلَٰئِكَ هُمُ ٱلْكَٰفِرُونَ ﴿٤٤﴾ (سورة المائدة: ٤٤)

❴Indeed, I did reveal the Torah in which was guidance and light, by which the prophets, who submitted to God's will, judged [the Jews]... and whoever does not judge by what Allah has revealed is a disbeliever,❵   *(Qur'an 5: 44)*

Jesus was also reported in the Gospel according to Matthew 9:16-17, to have made obedience to the divine laws the key to paradise: "**16** *Now behold, one came and said to him,'Good teacher, what good thing shall I do that I may have eternal life?'* **17** *So he said to him, 'Why do you call me good? No one is good but One, that is, God. But if you want to enter into life, keep the commandments.'*"[1] Also in Matthew 5:19, Jesus Christ was reported to have insisted on strict obedience to the commandments saying, "*Whoever therefore breaks one of the*

---

[1] *King James Version* and *The Authorized Version*.

least of these commandments, and teaches men so, shall be called least in the kingdom of heaven; but whoever does and teaches them, he shall be called great in the kingdom of heaven."

Divine law represents guidance for humankind in all walks of life. It defines right and wrong for them and offers human beings a complete system governing all of their affairs. The Creator alone knows best what is beneficial for His creation and what is not. Thus, the divine laws command and prohibit various acts and substances to protect the human spirit, the human body, and human society from harm. In order for human beings to fulfil their potential by living righteous lives, they need to worship God through obedience to His commandments.[2]

This was the religion conveyed in the message of Jesus; submission to the will of the one true God by obedience to His commandments. Jesus stressed to his followers that his mission did not cancel the laws received by Prophet Moses. As the prophets who came after Moses maintained the law, so did Jesus. Chapter *al-Mâ'idah*, verse 46 of the Qur'an indicates that Jesus confirmed the Laws of the Torah in his message.

﴿وَقَفَّيْنَا عَلَىٰٓ ءَاثَـٰرِهِم بِعِيسَى ٱبْنِ مَرْيَمَ مُصَدِّقًا لِّمَا بَيْنَ يَدَيْهِ مِنَ ٱلتَّوْرَىٰةِ وَءَاتَيْنَـٰهُ ٱلْإِنجِيلَ فِيهِ هُدًى وَنُورٌ وَمُصَدِّقًا لِّمَا بَيْنَ يَدَيْهِ مِنَ ٱلتَّوْرَىٰةِ ...﴾

(سورة المائدة: ٤٦)

﴿And in their footsteps, I sent Jesus, son of Mary, confirming the Torah that had come before him, and I gave him the Gospel, in which was guidance and light and confirmation of the Torah that had come before it,...﴾ *(Qur'an 5: 46)*

---

[2] *The Purpose of Creation*, Pp. 42-3.

In Matthew 5:17-18, Jesus stated: "**17** *Think not that I have come to abolish the law and the [way of] the prophets; I have come not to abolish them but to fulfil them.* **18** *For, I say to you, till heaven and earth pass away, not an iota, not a dot, will pass from the law until all is accomplished.*" However, Paul, who claimed to be a disciple of Jesus, systematically cancelled the laws. In his letter to the Romans, chapter 7:6, he stated, "*But now we are discharged from the law, dead to that which held us captive, so that we serve not under the old written code but in the new life of the Spirit.*"

Unitarianism

Jesus came as a prophet calling people to worship God alone, as the prophets before him did. God says in chapter *an-Nahl* (16):36, of the Qur'an:

$$ \text{﴿وَلَقَدْ بَعَثْنَا فِى كُلِّ أُمَّةٍ رَّسُولًا أَنِ اعْبُدُواْ اللَّهَ وَاجْتَنِبُواْ الطَّغُوتَ} $$

$$ ...﴿٣٦﴾﴾ \qquad (سورة النحل : ٣٦) $$

◁Surely, We[3] have sent to every nation a messenger [saying]: 'Worship Allah and avoid false gods...'▷   *(Qur'an 16: 36)*

In Luke 3:8, the Devil asks Jesus to worship him, promising him the authority and glory of all of the kingdoms of this world, "*And Jesus answered him, 'It is written, You shall worship the Lord your God, and him only shall you serve.*'" Thus, the essence of the message of Jesus was that only God alone deserves to be worshipped and that the worship of anyone or anything besides

---

[3] Literally "We", known as the "royal We" or the "majestic We" refers to Allah.

God or along with God is false. Jesus not only called people to this message but he also practically demonstrated it for them by bowing down in prayer and worshipping God himself. In Mark 14:32, it states: *"And they went to a place which was called Gethsemane; and he [Jesus] said to his disciples, 'Sit here, while I pray.'"* And in Luke 5:16, *"But he withdrew to the wilderness and prayed."*

Jesus called them to worship the one true God who is unique in His qualities. God does not have the attributes of His creation, nor does any creature share any of His attributes. In Matthew 19:16-17, when the man called Prophet Jesus "good" saying, *"Good teacher, what good thing shall I do that I may have eternal life?"* Prophet Jesus replied, *"Why do you call me good? No one is good but One, that is, God."* He denied the attribution of 'infinite goodness' or 'perfect goodness' to himself, and affirmed that this attribute belongs to Allah Alone.

The vast majority of Christians today pray to Jesus claiming that he is God. The Philosophers among them claim that they are not worshipping Jesus the man, but God who was manifest in Jesus the man. This is also the rationale of pagans who bow down in worship to idols. When a pagan philosopher is asked why he worships an idol which was made by human hands, he replies that he is not really worshipping the idol. Furthermore, he may claim that the idol is only a focal point for the presence of God, and thereby claim to be worshipping God who is manifest in the idol, and not the physical idol itself. There is little or no difference between that explanation and the answer given by Christians for worshipping Jesus. The origin of this deviation lies in the false belief that God is present in His creation. Such a belief justifies the worship of God's creation.

Jesus' message, which urged mankind to worship one God alone, became distorted after his departure. Later followers, beginning with Paul, turned that pure and simple message into a complicated trinitarian philosophy which justified the worship of Jesus, and then the worship of Jesus' mother, Mary,[4] the angels[5] and the saints. Catholics have a long list of saints to whom they turn in times of need. If something is lost, Saint Anthony of Thebes is prayed to in order to help find it.[6] St. Jude Thaddaeus is the patron saint of the impossible and is prayed to for intercession in incurable illnesses, unlikely marriages or the like.[7] The patron saint of travellers was Saint Christopher, to whom travellers used to pray for protection up until 1969, when he was officially struck off the list of saints by papal decree, after it was confirmed that he was fictitious.[8] Although he was officially crossed off the list of saints, there are many Catholics around the world today who are

---

[4] Called Saint Mary, she became an object of veneration in the Christian Church since the apostolic age. She was given the title *theotokos*, meaning "God-bearer" or "mother of God" in the 3rd or 4th century. Popular devotion to Mary — in the form of feasts, devotional services, and the rosary — has played a tremendously important role in the lives of Roman Catholics and the Orthodox. (*The New Encyclopaedia Britannica*, vol. 7, Pp. 897-8 and vol. 16, Pp. 278-9).

[5] The angels, Michael, Gabriel and Raphael were made saints and the religious celebration known as Michaelmas (called, "the Feast of St. Michael and All Saints" by the Anglicans) was dedicated to them on the 29th of September by the Western churches, and 8th of November by the Eastern Orthodox Church. The cult of St. Michael began in the Eastern Church in the 4th century. Because of St. Michael's traditional position as leader of the heavenly armies, veneration of all angels was eventually incorporated into his cult. (*The New Encyclopaedia Britannica*, vol. 8, p. 95). He became the patron saint of soldiers.

[6] *The World Book Encyclopedia*, vol. 1, p. 509.

[7] Ibid., vol. 11, p. 146.

[8] Ibid., vol. 3, p. 417.

still praying to St. Christopher.

Worshipping 'saints' contradicts and corrupts the worship of One God; and it is in vain, because neither the living nor the dead can answer the prayers of mankind. The worship of God should not be shared with His creation in any way, shape or form. In this regard, Allah said the following in Chapter *al-A'râf*, (7):194.

﴿إِنَّ الَّذِينَ تَدْعُونَ مِن دُونِ اللَّهِ عِبَادٌ أَمْثَالُكُمْ...﴾ (سورة الأعراف : ١٩٤)

{Surely, those whom you call on in prayer besides Allah are slaves like yourselves...}   *(Qur'an 7: 194)*

This was the message of Jesus Christ and all the prophets before him. It was also the message of the last prophet, Muhammad — may peace and blessings be upon all of them. Thus, if a Muslim or a person who calls himself a Muslim prays to a saint, he has stepped out of the bounds of Islam. Islam is not merely a belief, wherein one is only required to state that he or she believes that there is no God worthy of worship but Allah and that Muhammad was the last of the messengers, in order to attain paradise. This declaration of faith allows one who declares it to enter the doors of Islam, but there are many acts which may contradict this declaration and expel the doer from Islam as quickly as he or she came in. The most serious of those acts is praying to other than God.

Muslim not "Muhammadan"

Since Jesus' religion, and that of all of the earlier prophets, was the religion of submission to God, known in Arabic as *Islam,* his true followers were called submitters to God, known in Arabic as *Muslims.* In Islam, prayer is considered an act of worship. Prophet Muhammad (ﷺ) is reported to have said, "*Supplication is an act of worship."*[9] Consequently, Muslims do not accept being called Muhammadans, as followers of Christ are called Christians and followers of Buddha are called Buddhists. Christians worship Christ and Buddhists worship Buddha. The term Muhammadans implies that Muslims worship Muhammad, which is not the case at all. In the Qur'an, God chose the name *Muslim* for all who truly follow the prophets. The name *Muslim* in Arabic means "one who submits to the will of God."

﴿... هُوَ سَمَّىٰكُمُ ٱلْمُسْلِمِينَ مِن قَبْلُ وَفِي هَٰذَا ... ۝﴾   (سورة الحَجّ : ٧٨)

❨...It is He who named you Muslims both before and in this [scripture, the Qur'an]...❩   *(Qur'an 22: 78)*

Consequently, the essence of Jesus' message was that man should worship God alone. He should not be worshipped through his creation in any way. Thus, His image cannot be painted, carved or drawn. He is beyond human comprehension.

Images

Jesus did not condone the pagan practice of making images of God. He upheld the prohibition mentioned in the Torah, Exodus 20 verse 4: "*You shall not make for yourself a graven image, or any likeness of anything that is in heaven above, or that is in the earth beneath, or that is in the water under the earth.*" Consequently, the use of religious images, called icons,[10] was

---

[9] *Sunan Abu Dawood*, vol. 1, p. 387, no. 1474.

[10] The Iconoclastic Controversy was a dispute over the use of religious images (icons) in the Byzantine Empire in the 8th and 9th centuries. The Iconoclasts (those who rejected images) objected to icon worship for several reasons, including the Old Testament prohibition against images in the Ten=

firmly opposed by the early generation of Christian Scholars. However, in time, Greek and Roman tradition of image making and portraying God in human form eventually won out.

The prohibition is to prevent the eventual deterioration of worship of God into the worship of His creation. Once a human being makes a picture in his or her mind of God, the person is, in fact, trying to make God like His creation, because the human mind can only picture the things which it has seen, and God can not be seen in this life.

Christians with a tradition of worshipping through images often question how God can be worshipped without visualizing Him. God should be worshipped on the bases of the knowledge of

---

=Commandments (Ex. 20:4) and the possibility of idolatry. The defenders of icon worship insisted on the symbolic nature of images and on the dignity of created matter.

In the early church, the making and veneration of portraits of Christ and the saints were consistently opposed. The use of icons, nevertheless, steadily gained in popularity, especially in the eastern provinces of the Roman Empire. Toward the end of the 6th century CE and in the 7th, icons became the object of an officially encouraged cult, often implying a superstitious belief in their animation. Opposition to such practices became particularly strong in Asia Minor. In 726, the Byzantine emperor Leo III took a public stand against icons and by 730 their use was officially prohibited. This led to the persecution of icon worshippers that reached great severity in the reign of Leo's successor, Constantine V (741-775 CE.)

In 787 CE, however, the empress Irene convoked the seventh ecumenical council at Nicaea at which Iconoclasm was condemned and the use of images was reestablished. The Iconoclasts regained power in 814 after Leo V's accession, and the use of icons was again forbidden at a council (815 CE). The second Iconoclast period ended with the death of the emperor Theophilus in 842 CE. In 843 CE his widow finally restored icon veneration, an event still celebrated in the Eastern Orthodox Church as the Feast of Orthodoxy. (*The New Encyclopaedia Britannica*, vol. 6, p. 237)

His attributes which He revealed in authentic scripture. For example, Allah describes Himself in the Qur'an as being All-Merciful, so His worshippers should reflect on God's many mercies and give thanks to God for them. They should also contemplate on the nature of His mercy to them and show mercy to other human beings. Likewise, Allah refers to Himself as being Oft-Forgiving, so His worshippers should turn to Him in repentance and not give up hope when they commit sins. They should also appreciate God's forgiveness by being forgiving to other human beings.

Prophesy

Part of Prophet Jesus' message was to inform his followers of the prophet who would come after him. As John the Baptist heralded the coming of Jesus Christ, Jesus, in turn heralded the coming of the last of the prophets of God, Muhammad. In the Qur'an, chapter *aş-Şaff,* (61):6, God quotes Jesus' prophesy about Muhammad (ﷺ).

﴿وَإِذْ قَالَ عِيسَى ٱبْنُ مَرْيَمَ يَـٰبَنِىٓ إِسْرَٰٓءِيلَ إِنِّى رَسُولُ ٱللَّهِ إِلَيْكُم مُّصَدِّقًا لِّمَا بَيْنَ يَدَىَّ مِنَ ٱلتَّوْرَىٰةِ وَمُبَشِّرًا بِرَسُولٍ يَأْتِى مِنۢ بَعْدِى ٱسْمُهُۥٓ أَحْمَدُ ...﴿٦﴾ (سورة الصَّف : ٦)

﴿[Remember] when Jesus, son of Mary, said, 'Oh Children of Israel, I am the Messenger of Allah sent to you, confirming the Torah before me, and giving glad tidings of a Messenger coming after me, whose name will be Aḥmad[11] ...﴾   *(Qur'an 61: 6)*

---

[11] "Aḥmad" like "Muhammad" is a derivative from the Arabic root *ḥamd* meaning "praise; thanks". Prophet Muhammad (ﷺ) was also known by this name.

There are also some references in the Gospels which seem to refer to the coming of Prophet Muhammad — may God's peace and blessings be on all the prophets. In the Gospel according to John 14:16, Jesus is quoted as saying, "*And I will pray the Father, and he will give you another Counselor,* [12] *to be with you forever.*"

Christian laymen usually interpret the "Counselor" mentioned in John 14:16 as the Holy Spirit.[13] However, the phrase "*another Counselor*" implies that it will be someone else like Jesus and not the Holy Spirit.[14] Especially considering John 16:7, in which Jesus is reported to have said, "*Nevertheless I tell you the truth: it is to your advantage that I go away, for if I do not go away, the Counselor will not come to you; but if I go, I will send him to you.*" The term "Counselor" could not be referring to the Holy Spirit here, because — according to the Gospels — the Holy Spirit was already present in the world prior to Jesus' birth[15]

---

[12] The Greek word *paraclete* is translated as "Comforter" in the *King James Version*, and as "Advocate" and "Helper" in other translations. *Parakletos* means one who pleads the cause of another, one who counsels or advises another from deep concern for the other's welfare. (*Beacon Bible Commentary*, vol. 7, p. 168).

[13] See John 14:26, "*But the Counselor, the Holy Spirit, whom the Father will send in my name, he will teach you all things...*" However, in 1st John 4:1, the term "Spirit" is used to refer to prophet, "*Beloved, believe not every spirit, but try the spirits whether they are of God; because many false prophets are gone out into the world.*"

[14] In English, "another" may mean "one more of the *same* kind" or "one more of a *different* kind." The Greek text of the New Testament uses the word *allon*, which is the masculine accusative form of *allos*: "another of the *same* kind". The Greek word for "another of a different kind" is *heteros*, but the New Testament does not use this word in John 14:16. (*Jesus, A Prophet of Islam*, Pp. 15-6).

[15] John the Baptist was filled with the Holy Spirit while in his mother's womb (Luke 1:15); Elizabeth was filled with the Holy Spirit (Luke 1:41); John's=

as well as during his ministry.[16] This verse implies that the "Counselor" had not already come.

Jesus' declaration that prophet-counselor *"will be with you forever,"* could be interpreted to mean that there would be no need for additional prophets to succeed this Counselor. He would be the last of the Prophets of God, whose message would be preserved until the end of the world.[17]

Jesus' foretelling the coming of Muhammad — may God's peace be upon both of them — confirmed the prophesies about Prophet Muhammad (ﷺ) in the *Torah*. In Deuteronomy 18:18 & 19, it is written that the Lord said to Moses, *"I will raise up for them a prophet like you from among their brethren[18]; and I will put my words in his mouth[19], and he shall speak to them all that I command him. 19And whoever will not give heed to my words which he shall speak in my name[20], I myself will require it of him."* And in Isaiah 42, Isaiah prophesies about a chosen "Servant of the Lord" whose prophetic mission would be to all mankind, unlike the Hebrew prophets whose missions were limited to Israel. *"1 Behold my servant, whom I uphold, my chosen, in whom my soul delights; I have put my Spirit upon him, he will bring forth*

=father, Zacharias, was also filled with the Holy Spirit (Luke:1:67).

[16] The Holy Spirit was on Simeon (Luke 2:26) and it descended in the shape of a dove on Jesus (Luke 3: 22).

[17] *Jesus, A Prophet of Islam*, p. 13.

[18] The brethren of the Jews — who are themselves descendants of Abraham's son Isaac — are the Arabs; descendants of Isaac's brother Ishmael.

[19] The Qur'an literally means "the recital". Prophet Muhammad (ﷺ) taught that the Qur'an was the words of God. His own explanations and instructions are referred to as hadith.

[20] Each of the 114 chapters of the Qur'an begins with the prayer: "In the name of Allah, the Beneficent, the Most Merciful," except one; chapter 9.

justice to the nations... **4** *He will not fail or be discouraged till he has established justice in the earth; and the coastlands wait for his law....* **11** *Let the desert and its cities lift up their voice, the villages that Kedar inhabits.*" This particular servant of the Lord is the only one identified with *Kedar* [21], the Arabs.[22]

---

[21] Ishmael's descendants came to be known as Arabs, a term which, in Hebrew, meant those who inhabited the *'arabah* or desert (*Dictionary of the Bible*, p.47). The most prominently mentioned of Ishmael's twelve sons is Qaydar (*Kedar* in Hebrew). In some Bible verses Qaydar is synonymous with Arabs in general (Jeremiah 2:10; Ezekiel 27:21; Isaiah 60:7; Song of Solomon 1:5).

[22] *Jesus, A Prophet of Islam*, p. 11.

CHAPTER FOUR

THE WAY

he other aspect of Prophet Jesus' message was his invitation of people to follow his 'way'. Prophets brought divine laws or confirmed those brought by previous prophets, and invited people to worship God by obeying the divinely revealed laws. They also practically demonstrated for their followers, how one should live by the law. Consequently, they also invited those who believed in them to follow their way as the correct way to come close to God. This principle is enshrined in the Gospel according to John 14:6 : *"Jesus said to him, 'I am the way, and the truth, and the life; no one comes to the Father, but by me.'"* Although those who worship Jesus commonly quote this verse as part of the evidence for his divinity, Jesus did not invite people to worship himself instead of God, or as God. If these words were actually spoken by Jesus, what they mean is that one cannot worship God except in the way defined by the prophets of God. Jesus emphasized to his disciples, that they could only worship God by the way which he had taught them. In the Qur'an, chapter *Âl 'Imrân*, (3):31, God instructs Prophet Muhammad (ﷺ) to instruct mankind to follow him, if they truly love God:

﴿قُل إِن كُنتُمْ تُحِبُّونَ ٱللَّهَ فَٱتَّبِعُونِي يُحْبِبْكُمُ ٱللَّهُ وَيَغْفِرْ لَكُمْ ذُنُوبَكُمْ وَٱللَّهُ غَفُورٌ رَّحِيمٌ﴾

(سورة آل عِمرَان : ٣١)

﴾Tell [the people]: If you really love Allah, then follow me and Allah will love you and forgive your sins, for Allah is Oft-Forgiving, Most Merciful.﴿ *(Qur'an 3: 31)*

The way of the prophets is the only way to God, because it was prescribed by God Himself, and the purpose of the prophets was to convey Allah's instructions to mankind. Without prophets, people would not know how to worship Allah. Consequently, all prophets informed their followers of how to worship God. Conversely, adding anything to the religion brought by the prophets is incorrect.

Any changes made to the religion after the time of the prophets represent deviation inspired by Satan. In this regard, Prophet Muhammad (ﷺ) is reported to have said, *"Whoever adds anything new to the religion of Islam, will have it rejected (by God)."*[1] Furthermore, anyone who worshipped Allah contrary to Jesus' instructions, would have worshipped in vain.

Jesus' Way

First and foremost, it must be realized that Jesus Christ, the son of Mary, was the last in the line of Jewish prophets. He lived according to the *Torah,* the law of Moses, and taught his followers to do likewise. In Matthew 5:17-18, Jesus stated: **"17** *Think not that I have come to abolish the law and the [way of] the prophets;*

---

[1] Bukhari (Arabic-English), vol. 3, p. 535, hadith no. 861 and Muslim (English trans), vol. 3, p. 931, hadith no. 4266.

I have come not to abolish them but to fulfil them. **18** *For, I say to you, till heaven and earth pass away, not an iota, not a dot, will pass from the law until all is accomplished.*" Unfortunately, about five years after the end of Jesus' ministry, a young rabbi by the name of Saul of Tarsus, who claimed to have seen Jesus in a vision, began to change Jesus' way. Paul (his Roman name) had considerable respect for Roman philosophy and he spoke proudly of his own Roman citizenship. His conviction was that non-Jews who became Christians should not be burdened with the *Torah* in any respect. The author of Acts 13:39 quotes Paul as saying, "*And by him every one that believes is freed from everything from which you could not be freed by the law of Moses.*" It was primarily through the efforts of Paul that the Church began to take on its non-Jewish character. Paul[2] wrote most of the New Testament letters (epistles), which the Church accepts as the official doctrine and inspired Scripture. These letters do not preserve the Gospel of Jesus or even represent it;[3] instead, Paul transformed the teachings of Christ into a Hellenic (Greco-Roman) philosophy.

The following are some examples of teachings which Prophet Jesus followed and taught, but which were later abandoned by the Church. However, most of these teachings were revived in the final message of Islam brought by Prophet Muhammad (ﷺ) and remain a fundamental part of Muslim religious practices until today.

Circumcision

Jesus was circumcised. According to the *Old Testament*, this tradition began with Prophet Abraham, who was himself neither a

---

[2] He was beheaded in Rome 34 years after the end of Jesus' ministry.

[3] *Biblical Studies From a Muslim Perspective*, p. 18.

Jew nor a Christian. In Genesis 17:10, it is written, "**9** *And God said to Abraham, 'As for you, you shall keep my covenant, you and your descendants after you throughout their generations.* **10** *This is my covenant, which you shall keep, between me and you and your descendants after you:* <u>*Every male among you shall be circumcised.*</u> **11** *You shall be circumcised in the flesh of your foreskins and it shall be a sign of the covenant between me and you.* **12** <u>*He that is eight days old among you shall be circumcised;*</u> *every male throughout your generations, whether born in your house, or bought with your money from any foreigner who is not of your offspring,* **13** *both he that is born in your house and he that is bought with your money, shall be circumcised.* <u>*So shall my covenant be in your flesh an everlasting covenant.*</u>*' "*

In the Gospel according to Luke 2:21 : *"And at the end of eight days, when he was circumcised, he was called Jesus, the name given by the angel before he was conceived in the womb."* Consequently, to be circumcised was a part of Jesus' way. However, today most Christians are not circumcised, because of a rationale introduced by Paul. He claimed that circumcision was the circumcision of the heart. In his letter to the Romans 2:29, he wrote: *"He is a Jew who is one inwardly, and* <u>*real circumcision is a matter of the heart, spiritual and not literal.*</u>*"* In his letter to the Galatians 5:2, he wrote: *"Now I, Paul, say to you that if you* <u>*receive circumcision, Christ will be of no advantage to you.*</u>*"* [4] This was Paul's false interpretation. On the other hand, Jesus was not circumcised by the heart nor did he say anything about circumcision of the heart, he kept the "everlasting covenant" and was circumcised in the flesh. Thus, an important part of following the way of Jesus is circumcision.

---

[4] See also Galatians 6:15.

Prophet Muhammad (ﷺ) is quoted as saying, *"There are five practices which constitute the prophetic way[5]: circumcision, shaving pubic hair and underarm hair, clipping fingernails and toenails; and trimming the moustache."*[6]

Pork

Jesus did not eat pork. He followed the laws of Moses and he did not eat pork. In Leviticus 11:7-8, *"7 And the swine, because it parts the hoof and is cloven-footed but does not chew the cud, is unclean to you. 8 Of their flesh you shall not eat, and their carcasses you shall not touch; they are unclean to you."*[7] Jesus' only dealing with pigs was his permission to the unclean spirits which were possessing a man, to enter them. When they entered the herd of pigs, they ran into the water and drowned. However, most people who call themselves Christians today not only eat pork, they love it so much that they have made pigs the subject of nursery rhymes (e.g. This little piggy went to market...) and children's stories (e.g. The Three Little Pigs). Porky Pig is very popular cartoon character and recently a full-length feature movie was made about a pig called "Babe". Thus, it may be said that those who call themselves followers of Christ are not in fact following the way of Christ.

In Islamic law, the prohibition of pork and its products is strictly maintained, from the time of Prophet Muhammad (ﷺ) until today. In the Qur'an, chapter *al-Baqarah*, (2):173 God says:

---

[5] The Arabic term used is *fiṭrah* which literally means nature.

[6] Bukhari (Arabic-English), vol.7, p. 515, hadith no. 777 and Muslim (English trans), vol.1, p. 159, hadith no. 495.

[7] See also, Deuteronomy 14:8.

$$\text{﴿إِنَّمَا حَرَّمَ عَلَيْكُمُ الْمَيْتَةَ وَالدَّمَ وَلَحْمَ الْخِنزِيرِ وَمَا أُهِلَّ بِهِ لِغَيْرِ اللَّهِ فَمَنِ اضْطُرَّ غَيْرَ بَاغٍ وَلَا عَادٍ فَلَا إِثْمَ عَلَيْهِ إِنَّ اللَّهَ غَفُورٌ رَّحِيمٌ ﴾}$$

(سورة البَقَرَة: ١٧٣)

﴾He has only forbidden you animals which die of themselves, blood, and swine, and animals sacrificed for others besides Allah. But if one is forced by necessity and not wilful disobedience nor transgression, then there is no sin on him. Truly, Allah is Oft-Forgiving, Most Merciful.﴿ [8]

(Qur'an 2: 173)

Blood

Jesus also did not eat anything containing blood, nor did he eat blood. God is recorded as instructed Prophet Moses in the *Torah,* Deuteronomy 12:16, *"Only you shall not eat the blood; you shall pour it upon the earth like water,"* and in Leviticus 19:26, *"You shall not eat any flesh with the blood in it. You shall not practice augury or witchcraft."* This prohibition has been preserved in the final revelation, chapter *al-An'âm* (6):145 until today.

$$\text{﴿قُل لَّا أَجِدُ فِي مَا أُوحِيَ إِلَيَّ مُحَرَّمًا عَلَى طَاعِمٍ يَطْعَمُهُ إِلَّا أَن يَكُونَ مَيْتَةً أَوْ دَمًا مَّسْفُوحًا أَوْ لَحْمَ خِنزِيرٍ فَإِنَّهُ رِجْسٌ ...﴾}$$

(سورة الأنعَام: ١٤٥)

﴾Say [O' Muhammad]: I do not find in what has been revealed to me anything forbidden to be eaten by one who wishes to eat, except for animals which die of themselves, flowing blood, and swine flesh, for they are indeed impure...﴿

(Qur'an 6: 145)

---

[8] See also chapter *al-Mâ'idah*, (5): 3.

Consequently, particular rites of slaughter were prescribed by God for all the nations to whom prophets were sent, in order to ensure that most of the blood was effectively removed from the slaughtered animals and to remind human beings of God's bounties. The Qur'an refers to these instructions in chapter al-Ḥajj (22):34 as follows:

﴿وَلِكُلِّ أُمَّةٍ جَعَلْنَا مَنسَكًا لِّيَذْكُرُوا اسْمَ اللَّهِ عَلَى مَا رَزَقَهُم مِّن بَهِيمَةِ الْأَنْعَمِ... ﴿٣٤﴾﴾

(سورة الحجّ : ٣٤)

﴿For every nation I have appointed rites of slaughter in order that they may mention Allah's name over the cattle He has provided them...﴾   *(Qur'an 22: 34)*

Jesus and his early followers observed the proper method of slaughter by mentioning God's name and cutting the jugular veins of the animals while they were living to allow the heart to pump out the blood. However, Christians today do not attach much importance to proper slaughter methods, as prescribed by God.

Alcohol

Jesus consecrated himself to God and therefore abstained from alcoholic drinks according to the instructions recorded in Numbers 6:1-4 : "*And the Lord said to Moses,* **2** '*Say to the people of Israel, When either a man or a woman makes a special vow, the vow of the Nazirite,*[9] *to separate himself to the Lord,* **3** he shall separate himself from wine and strong drink; *he shall drink no vinegar made from wine or strong drink, and shall not drink any juice of grapes or eat grapes, fresh or dried.* **4** *All the days of his*

---

[9] That is *one separated* or *one consecrated*.

separation he shall eat nothing that is produced by the grapevine, not even the seeds or the skins.'"

In the Qur'an, chapter *al-Mâ'idah* (5):90, Allah prohibits intoxicants irrevocably.

﴿يَـٰٓأَيُّهَا ٱلَّذِينَ ءَامَنُوٓا۟ إِنَّمَا ٱلۡخَمۡرُ وَٱلۡمَيۡسِرُ وَٱلۡأَنصَابُ وَٱلۡأَزۡلَـٰمُ رِجۡسٌ مِّنۡ عَمَلِ ٱلشَّيۡطَـٰنِ فَٱجۡتَنِبُوهُ لَعَلَّكُمۡ تُفۡلِحُونَ ٩﴾   (سورة المائدة: ٩٠)

❬O' you who believe, intoxicants, gambling, sacrificial altars, and divination are an abomination of Satan's handiwork. So avoid it in order to be successful.❭   *(Qur'an 5: 90)*

As to the 'miracle of turning water into wine',[10] it is found only in the Gospel of John, which consistently contradicts the other three gospels. As mentioned earlier, the Gospel of John was opposed as heretical in the early Church[11], while the other three Gospels were referred to as the Synoptic Gospels, because the texts contained a similar treatment of Jesus' life.[12] Consequently, New Testament scholars have expressed doubt about the authenticity of this incident.

Ablution before prayer

Prior to making formal prayer, Jesus used to wash his limbs according to the teachings of the Torah. Moses and Aaron are recorded as doing the same in Exodus 40:30-1, "**30** *And he set the laver between the tent of meeting and the altar, and put water in it for washing,* **31** *with which Moses and Aaron and his sons washed*

---

[10] John 2:1-11.

[11] *The Five Gospels*, p. 20.

[12] *The New Encyclopaedia Britannica*, vol. 5, p. 379.

their hands and their feet.... as the Lord commanded Moses."

In the Qur'an, chapter *al-Mâ'idah*, (5):6, ablution for prayer
is prescribed as follows:

$$\text{﴿يَـٰٓأَيُّهَا ٱلَّذِينَ ءَامَنُوٓاْ إِذَا قُمۡتُمۡ إِلَى ٱلصَّلَوٰةِ فَٱغۡسِلُواْ وُجُوهَكُمۡ وَأَيۡدِيَكُمۡ}$$
$$\text{إِلَى ٱلۡمَرَافِقِ وَٱمۡسَحُواْ بِرُءُوسِكُمۡ وَأَرۡجُلَكُمۡ إِلَى ٱلۡكَعۡبَيۡنِ ...﴿٦﴾}$$

(سورة المائدة : ٦)

❴O' you who believe, when you intend to pray, wash your faces
and fore-arms up to the elbows, wipe your heads and wash your
feet up to the ankles...❵　　　　　　　　　　　*(Qur'an 5: 6)*

Prostration in prayer

Jesus is described in the Gospels as prostrating during prayer.
In Matthew 26:39, the author describes an incident which took
place when Jesus went with his disciples to Gethsemane: *"And
going a little farther he fell on his face and prayed, 'My Father, if
it be possible, let this cup pass from me; nevertheless, not as I will,
but as thou wilt.'"*

Christians today kneel down, clasping their hands, in a
posture which cannot be ascribed to Jesus. The method of
prostration in prayer followed by Jesus, was not of his own
making. It was the mode of prayer of the prophets before him. In
the Old Testament, Genesis 17:3, Prophet Abraham is recorded to
have fallen on his face in prayer; in Numbers 16:22 & 20:6, both
Moses and Aaron are recorded to have fallen on their faces in
worship; in Joshua 5:14 & 7:6, Joshua fell on his face to the earth
and worshipped; in 1 Kings 18:42, Elijah bowed down on the
ground and put his face between his knees. This was the way of

the prophets through whom God chose to convey His word to the world. And it is only by this way that those who claim to follow Jesus will gain the salvation which he preached in his Gospel.

Chapter *al-Insân*, (76):25-6, is only one of many Qur'anic examples of God's instructions to the believers to bow down in worship to Him.

﴿وَٱذْكُرِ ٱسْمَ رَبِّكَ بُكْرَةً وَأَصِيلًا ۝ وَمِنَ ٱلَّيْلِ فَٱسْجُدْ لَهُ وَسَبِّحْهُ لَيْلًا طَوِيلًا ۝﴾

(سورة الإنسان: ٢٥-٢٦)

﴿Remember the Name of your Lord in the morning and evening, and prostrate for Him and glorify him for a long time nightly.﴾

(Qur'an 76: 25-26)

Veiling

The women around Jesus veiled themselves according to the practice of women around the earlier prophets. Their garments were loose and covered their bodies completely, and they wore scarves which covered their hair. In Genesis 24:64-5 : *"And Rebekah lifted up her eyes, and when she saw Isaac, she alighted from the camel, 65 and said to the servant, 'Who is the man yonder, walking in the field to meet us?' The servant said, 'It is my master.' So she took her veil and covered herself."* Paul wrote in his first letter to the Corinthians, *"5 But any woman who prays or prophesies with her head unveiled dishonours her head — it is the same as if her head were shaven. 6 For if a woman will not veil herself, then she should cut off her hair; but if it is disgraceful for a woman to be shorn or shaven, let her wear a veil."* Some may argue that it was the general custom of those times to be completely veiled. However, that is not the case. In both Rome and Greece, whose cultures dominated the region, the popular dress was quite short and revealed the arms, legs and chest. Only religious women in Palestine, following Jewish tradition, covered themselves modestly.

According to Rabbi Dr. Menachem M. Brayer (Professor of Biblical Literature at Yeshiva University), it was customary that Jewish women went out in public with a head covering which, sometimes, even covered the whole face leaving only one eye free.[13] He further stated that "during the Tannaitic period, the Jewish woman's failure to cover her head was considered an affront to her modesty. When her head was uncovered she might be fined four hundred zuzims for this offence."[14]

The famous early Christian theologian, St. Tertullian (d. 220 CE), in his famous treatise 'On The Veiling of Virgins' wrote, "Young women, you wear your veils out on the streets, so you should wear them in the church, you wear them when you are among strangers, then wear them among your brothers..." Among the Canon laws of the Catholic church until today, there is a law that requires women to cover their heads in church.[15] Christian denominations, such as the Amish and the Menonites for example, keep their women veiled to the present day.

In the Qur'an, chapter *an-Noor*, (24):31, the believing women are instructed to cover their charms and wear veils on their heads and chests.

---

[13] *The Jewish Woman in Rabbinic Literature*, p. 239.

[14] Ibid., p. 139.

[15] Clara M. Henning, "Canon Law and the Battle of the Sexes" in *Religion and Sexism*, p. 272.

وَقُل لِّلْمُؤْمِنَٰتِ يَغْضُضْنَ مِنْ أَبْصَٰرِهِنَّ وَيَحْفَظْنَ فُرُوجَهُنَّ وَلَا يُبْدِينَ زِينَتَهُنَّ
إِلَّا مَا ظَهَرَ مِنْهَا ۖ وَلْيَضْرِبْنَ بِخُمُرِهِنَّ عَلَىٰ جُيُوبِهِنَّ ۖ ... (٣١) ﴿ (سورة النور: ٣١)

❮Tell the believing women to lower their gaze and protect their private parts and not to expose their adornment except only what normally shows, and to draw their head-scarves over their bosoms...❯ *(Qur'an 24: 31)*

In chapter *al-Aḥzâb* (33): 59, the reason for veiling is given. Allah states that it makes the believing women known in the society and provides protection for them from possible social harm.

Greetings

Jesus greeted his followers by saying "Peace be upon you". In chapter 20:19, the anonymous author of the Gospel according to John wrote the following about Jesus after his supposed crucifixion: *"Jesus said to them again, 'Peace be with you. As the Father has sent me, even so I send you.'"* This greeting was according to that of the prophets as mentioned in the books of the Old Testament. For example, in 1st Samuel 25:6, Prophet David instructed emissaries whom he sent to Nabal: *"And thus you shall salute him: 'Peace be to you, and peace be to your house, and peace be to all that you have.'"* The Qur'an instructs all who enter homes to give greetings of peace;[16] and those entering Paradise will be greeted similarly by the angels.[17] In chapter *al-An'âm*, (6):54, God instructs the believers to greet each other with peace:

---

[16] Chapter *an-Noor*, (24):27.

[17] Chapter *al-A'râf*, (7):46.

﴾وَإِذَا جَاءَكَ ٱلَّذِينَ يُؤْمِنُونَ بِـَٔايَـٰتِنَا فَقُلْ سَلَـٰمٌ عَلَيْكُمْ ... ﴿٥٤﴾﴾

(سورة الأنعام: ٥٤)

﴾When those who believe in my signs come to you, greet them: Peace be upon you...﴿   *(Qur'an 6: 54)*

Compulsory Charity

Jesus confirmed the institution of compulsory charity known as "the tithe (tenth)", which was required from the annual harvest to be given back to God in celebration. In Deuteronomy 14:22: *"You shall tithe all the yield of your seed, which comes forth from the field year by year."*

In the 6th chapter, *al-An'âm*, verse 141, God reminds the believers to pay the charity at the time of harvest:

﴾۞ وَهُوَ ٱلَّذِى أَنشَأَ جَنَّـٰتٍ مَّعْرُوشَـٰتٍ وَغَيْرَ مَعْرُوشَـٰتٍ وَٱلنَّخْلَ وَٱلزَّرْعَ مُخْتَلِفًا أُكُلُهُ وَٱلزَّيْتُونَ وَٱلرُّمَّانَ مُتَشَـٰبِهًا وَغَيْرَ مُتَشَـٰبِهٍ كُلُواْ مِن ثَمَرِهِۦ إِذَآ أَثْمَرَ وَءَاتُواْ حَقَّهُۥ يَوْمَ حَصَادِهِۦ وَلَا تُسْرِفُوٓاْ إِنَّهُۥ لَا يُحِبُّ ٱلْمُسْرِفِينَ ﴿١٤١﴾﴾

(سورة الأنعام: ١٤١)

﴾It is He who produces trellised and un-trellised gardens, date palms and crops of different shape and taste; and olives and pomegranates, similar yet different. Eat of their fruit when they yield, but pay the due[18] at the time of harvest without being extravagant, for surely He does not like those who are extravagant.﴿   *(Qur'an 6: 141)*

---

[18] One tenth if the field is naturally irrigated and one twentieth if it is artificially irrigated.

The system of compulsory charity (in Arabic, *zakâh*) is well organized with different rates for cash and precious metals than that for agricultural products and cattle. Also those who are eligible to receive are clearly defined in the Qur'an, chapter *at-Tawbah* (9):60. It is mainly distributed among various categories of the poor and is not used to provide a comfortable living for priests.

Fasting

According to the Gospels, Jesus fasted for forty days. Matthew 4:2: *"And he fasted forty days and forty nights, and afterward he was hungry."*[19] This was in accordance with the practice of the earlier prophets. Moses is also recorded in Exodus 34:28, to have fasted: *"And he was there with the Lord forty days and forty nights; he neither ate bread nor drank water. And he wrote upon the tables the words of the covenant, the ten commandments."*

In the Qur'an, chapter *al-Baqarah*, (2):183, the believers are instructed to observe regular fasting.

﴿يَٰٓأَيُّهَا ٱلَّذِينَ ءَامَنُوا۟ كُتِبَ عَلَيْكُمُ ٱلصِّيَامُ كَمَا كُتِبَ عَلَى ٱلَّذِينَ مِن قَبْلِكُمْ لَعَلَّكُمْ تَنَّقُونَ ۝﴾ (سورة البَقَرَة: ١٨٣)

◊O' you who believe, fasting is prescribed for you as it was prescribed for those before you, in order that you may become pious.◊   *(Qur'an 2: 183)*

The purpose of fasting is clearly defined as being for the development of God-consciousness. Only God knows who is

---

[19] See also Matthew 6:16 and 17:21.

actually fasting and who is not. Consequently, one who is fasting refrains from eating and drinking based on awareness of God. Regular fasting heightens that awareness which subsequently leads to a greater inclination towards righteousness.

The believers are required to fast from dawn until dusk for the whole month of Ramaḍân (the ninth month of the Islamic - Hijri calendar). Prophet Muhammad (ﷺ) also said, *"The best fast (outside of Ramaḍân) is that of my brother (Prophet) David who used to fast every other day."*[20]

Interest

Prophet Jesus opposed interest because the texts of the *Torah* expressly forbade interest. It is recorded in Deuteronomy 23:19 that, *"You shall not lend upon interest to your brother, interest on money, interest upon victuals,*[21] *interest on anything that is lent for interest."*[22] Interest is also strictly forbidden in chapter *al-Baqarah* (2):278 of the Qur'an:

﴿يَٰٓأَيُّهَا ٱلَّذِينَ ءَامَنُوا۟ ٱتَّقُوا۟ ٱللَّهَ وَذَرُوا۟ مَا بَقِىَ مِنَ ٱلرِّبَوٰٓا۟ إِن كُنتُم مُّؤۡمِنِينَ ۝﴾

(سورة البَقَرَة: ٢٧٨)

❨O' you who believe, fear Allah and give up what interest remains due to you, if you really are believers.❩   *(Qur'an 2: 278)*

---

[20] Bukhari (Arabic-English), vol. 3, Pp. 113-4, no. 200 and Muslim (English trans), Vol. 2, p. 565, no. 2595.

[21] Food or provisions.

[22] However, in the verse following this one, the Jews made permissible lending on interest to non-Jews: *"To a foreigner you may lend upon interest, but to your brother you shall not lend upon interest."* (Deuteronomy 23:20)

In order to fulfil this divine requirement, Muslims developed an alternative system of banking, commonly known as 'Islamic Banking', which is interest-free.

Polygamy

There is no record of Prophet Jesus opposing polygamy. To do so would be to condemn the practice of the prophets before him. There are a number of examples of polygamous marriages among the prophets recorded in the *Torah*. Prophet Abraham had two wives according to Genesis 16:13 *"So after Abram had dwelt ten years in the land of Canaan, Sarah, Abram's wife, took Hagar the Egyptian, her maid, and gave her to Abram her husband as a wife."* So did Prophet David, according to the first book of Samuel 27:3, *"And David dwelt with Achish at Gat, he and his men, every man with his household, and David with his two wives, Ahin'o-am of Jezreel, and Abigail of Carmel, Nabal's widow."* In 1st Kings 11:3, Solomon is said to have *"...had seven hundred wives, princesses, and three hundred concubines; and his wives turned away his heart."* Solomon's son, Rehobo'am, also had a number of wives, according to 2nd Chronicles 11:21, *"Rehobo'am loved Ma'acah the daughter of Absalom above all his wives and concubines (he took eighteen wives and sixty concubines, and had twenty-eight sons and sixty daughters)."* In fact, the *Torah* even specified laws regarding the division of inheritance in polygamous circumstances. In Deuteronomy 21:15-16, the law states: *"15 If a man has two wives, the one loved and the other disliked, and they have borne him children, both the loved and the disliked, and if the first-born son is hers that is disliked, 16 then on the day when he assigns his possessions as an inheritance to his sons, he may not treat the son of the loved as the first-born in preference to the son of the disliked, who is the first-born.*" The only restriction on polygamy was the ban on taking a wife's sister as a rival wife in Leviticus 18: 18, "*And you shall not take a woman as a rival wife to her sister, uncovering her nakedness while her sister is yet alive.*" The Talmud advises a maximum of four wives as was the practice of Prophet Jacob.[23]

According to Father Eugene Hillman, "No-where in the New Testament is there any explicit commandment that marriage should be monogamous or any explicit commandment forbidding polygamy."[24] He further stressed the fact that the Church in Rome banned polygamy in order to conform to Greco-Roman culture which prescribed only one legal wife while tolerating concubinage and prostitution.[25]

Islam limited polygamy to a maximum of four wives at one time and stipulated the maintenance of justice as a basic condition for polygamy. In chapter *an-Nisâ'* (4):3, God states:

﴿... فَٱنكِحُوا۟ مَا طَابَ لَكُم مِّنَ ٱلنِّسَاءِ مَثْنَىٰ وَثُلَـٰثَ وَرُبَـٰعَ فَإِنْ خِفْتُمْ أَلَّا تَعْدِلُوا۟ فَوَٰحِدَةً

(سورة النِّسَاء : ٣)   ... ﴿۳﴾﴾

❨...Marry of the women that please you; two, three or four. But if you fear that you will not be able to deal justly, then [marry only] one...❩
                                                    (Qur'an 4: 3)

---

[23] *Women in Judaism*, p. 148.

[24] *Polygamy Reconsidered*, p. 140.

[25] Ibid., p. 17.

CONCLUSION

There is only One God, Who created the whole human race and communicated to them one message: submission to the will of God — known in Arabic as Islam. That message was conveyed to the first human beings on this earth, and reaffirmed by all of the prophets of God who came after them, down through the ages. The essence of the message of Islam was that humans should worship only One God by obeying His commandments, and should avoid worshipping God's creation in any way, shape or form.

Jesus Christ, born of the Virgin Mary, performed miracles and invited the Israelites to the same message of submission (Islam), as did all of the prophets who preceded him. He was not God, nor was he the 'Son of God', but was the Messiah, an illustrious prophet of God. Jesus did not invite people to worship himself; rather, he called them to worship God and he himself worshipped God. He confirmed the laws of the *Torah* which Prophet Moses taught, he lived by them, and instructed his disciples to follow them to the finest detail. Before his departure, he informed his followers of the last Prophet, Muhammad of Arabia (ﷺ), who would come after him, and instructed them to observe his teachings.

In the generations after Jesus' departure from this world, his teachings were distorted and he was elevated to the status of God. Six centuries later, with the coming of Prophet Muhammad (ﷺ), the truth about Jesus Christ was finally retold and preserved eternally in the last book of divine revelation, the Qur'an.

Furthermore, the laws of Moses, which Jesus followed, were revived in their pure and unadulterated form, and implemented in the divinely prescribed way of life known as Islam.

Consequently, the reality of the prophets, their uniform message, and the way of life which they followed, can only be found preserved in the religion of Islam, the only religion prescribed by God for man. Furthermore, only Muslims today actually follow Jesus and his true teachings. Their way of life is much more in tune with the way of life of Jesus than any of the modern day "Christians". Love and respect of Jesus Christ is an article of faith in Islam. Allah stressed the importance of belief in Jesus in numerous places in the Qur'an. For example, in Chapter *an-Nisâ* (4): 159, He said:

وَإِن مِّنْ أَهْلِ ٱلْكِتَبِ إِلَّا لَيُؤْمِنَنَّ بِهِۦ قَبْلَ مَوْتِهِۦ وَيَوْمَ ٱلْقِيَمَةِ يَكُونُ عَلَيْهِمْ شَهِيدًا ﴿١٥٩﴾ (النِّسَاء: ١٥٩)

{And all of the people of the scripture must believe in him [Jesus] before his death, and on the Day of Resurrection, he will be a witness against them.} *(Qur'an 4: 159)*

Jesus' Return

Even the expected return of Jesus, which Christians are awaiting, is a part of the Islamic faith. However, he will not return to judge the world as modern Christians believe, because judgement only belongs to God. The Qur'an teaches that Jesus was not killed by the Jews, but was instead raised up alive by God into the heavens.

وَقَوْلِهِمْ إِنَّا قَتَلْنَا ٱلْمَسِيحَ عِيسَى ٱبْنَ مَرْيَمَ رَسُولَ ٱللَّهِ وَمَا قَتَلُوهُ وَمَا صَلَبُوهُ وَلَٰكِن

شُبِّهَ لَهُمْ وَإِنَّ ٱلَّذِينَ ٱخْتَلَفُوا فِيهِ لَفِى شَكٍّ مِّنْهُ مَا لَهُم بِهِۦ مِنْ عِلْمٍ إِلَّا ٱتِّبَاعَ ٱلظَّنِّ وَمَا

قَتَلُوهُ يَقِينَا ۝ بَل رَّفَعَهُ ٱللَّهُ إِلَيْهِ وَكَانَ ٱللَّهُ عَزِيزًا حَكِيمًا ۝

(النساء : ١٥٧–١٥٨)

❨And their [the Jews'] saying: 'We killed the Mesiah, Jesus son of Mary,' but they did not kill him, nor did they crucify him, rather it was made to seem that way to them. And those who differ about it are full of doubts. They are of no knowledge about it, and follow instead conjecture. They certainly did not kill him, [for], Allah raised him up to himself. And Allah is All-Powreful, All-Wise.❩

(Qur'an 4: 157-158)

Among the things which Prophet Muhammad (ﷺ) is recorded to have said regarding Prophet Jesus' return is the following, *"There will be no prophet between me and Jesus, and he will return. When he does, you will know him. He will be a well-built man of ruddy complexion and he will descend wearing a two-piece garment. His hair will look wet, though no water touched it. He will fight people to establish Islam and he will break the cross, kill the pig and cancel the jizyah.*[26] *During his time, Allah will destroy all religions except Islam and the False-Christ will be killed. Jesus will remain on earth for forty years, and when he dies, Muslims will pray the funeral prayer for him."* [27]

Jesus' return will be one of the signs of the coming of the Day of Judgement.

---

[26] The tax taken from Christians and Jews living under Muslim rule in lieu of *zakâh* (compulsory charity) and military service.

[27] *Sunan Abu Dawood*, vol. 3, p. 1203, hadith no. 4310 and authenticated by Shaykh al-Albâni in *Saheeh Sunan Abi Dawood*, vol. 3, p. 815-6, hadith no. 3635.

BIBLIOGRAPHY

Arberry, Arthur J., *The Koran Interpreted,* London: George Allen & Unwin, 1980.

Barr, James, "Abba Isn't "Daddy'," in *Journal of Theological Studies,* vol. 39, 1988.

————, "Abba, Father", in *Theology,* vol. 91, no. 741, 1988.

Brayer, Menachem M., *The Jewish Woman in Rabbinic Literature: A Psychosocial Perspective,* Hoboken, N.J: Ktav Publishing House, 1986.

Burton, John, *An Introduction to the Hadith,* UK: Edinburgh University Press, 1994.

————, *The Collection of the Qur'an,* Cambridge: Cambridge University Press, 1977.

Cragg, Kenneth, *The Mind of the Qur'an,* London: George Allen & Unwin, 1973.

Dīdat, Aḥmed, *Christ in Islam,* Durban, South Africa: The Islamic Propagation Centre, n.d.

Dunn, James, *Christology in the Making,* London: SCM Press, and Philadelphia: Westminster Press, 1980.

Friedman, Richard, *Who Wrote the Bible?,* U.S.A.: Summit Books, 1987.

Funk, Robert W., Roy W. Hoover and The Jesus Seminar, *The Five Gospels,* New York: Polebridge Press, Macmillan Publishing Co., 1993.

Graham, William, *Beyond the Written Word,* UK: Cambridge University Press, 1993.

Ḥamidullah, Mohammed, *Muhammad Rasulullah,* Lahore, Pakistan: Idara-e-Islamiat, n.d.

Ḥasan, Aḥmad, *Sunan Abu Dawood,* (English Trans.), Lahore: Sh. Muhammad Ashraf Publishers, 1st ed., 1987.

Hastings, J., *Dictionary of the Bible,* New York: Chas. Scribner's Sons, revised ed., 1963.

Hebblethwaite, Brian, *The Incarnation,* England: Cambridge University Press, 1987.

Hick John, ed., *The Myth of God Incarnate,* London: SCM Press Ltd., 1977.

————, *The Metaphor of god Incarnate,* London: SCM Press Ltd, 1993.

Hillman, Eugene, *Polygamy Reconsidered: African Plural Marriage and the Christian Churches*, New York: Orbis Books, 1975.

Hornby, A.S., *The Oxford Advanced Learner's Dictionary,* England: Oxford University Press, 4th ed., 1989.

Khan, Muhammad Muḥsin, *Ṣaḥeeḥ al-Bukhari*, (Arabic-English), Lahore: Kazi Publications, 6th ed., 1986.

Gibb, H.A.R. and J.H. Kramers, *Shorter Encyclopaedia of Islam,* Ithaca, New York: Cornell University Press, 1953.

Maccoby, Hyam, *The Myth-maker: Paul and the Invention of Christianity,* New York: Harper & Row, 1987.

Mayfield, Joseph H., *Beacon Bible Commentary,* Kansas City: Beacon Hill Press, 1965.

Moule, C.F.D., *The Origin of Christology,* U.K.: Cambridge University Press, 1977.

Mufassir, Sulaymân Shahid, *Biblical Studies from a Muslim Perspective,* Washington: The Islamic Center, 1973.

—————————, *Jesus, A Prophet of Islam,* Indianapolis: American Trust Publications, 1980.

Nicholson, Reynold A., *Literary History of the Arabs,* Cambridge: Cambridge University Press.

Philips, Abu Ameenah Bilal, *The Purpose of Creation,* Sharjah, U.A.E.: Dar Al Fatah, 1995.

Ramsey, Michael, *Jesus and the Living Past,* UK: Oxford University Press, 1980.

Ruether, Rosemary R., ed., *Religion and Sexism: Images of Woman in the Jewish and Christian Traditions,* New York: Simon and Schuster, 1974.

Spray, Lisa, *Jesus,* Tucson, AZ: Renaissance Productions, 1987.

Ṣiddiqi, 'Abdul Ḥamid, *Ṣaḥeeḥ Muslim,* (English Trans.), Lahore: Sh. Muhammad Ashraf Publishers, 1987.

The New Encyclopaedia Britannica, Chicago: Encyclopaedia Britannica, Inc., 15th Edition, 1991.

The World Book Encyclopedia, Chicago: World Book, Inc., 1987.

SYMBOLS' DIRECTORY

(ﷻ) : *Subḥânahu wa Ta'âla* — "The Exalted."

(ﷺ) : *Ṣalla-Allâhu 'Alayhi wa Sallam* — "Blessings and peace be upon him."

(ﷺ) : *'Alayhis-Salâm* — "May peace be upon him."

(ﷺ) : *Raḍia-Allâhu 'Anhu* — "May Allah be pleased with him."